THE REFORM OF ADVANCED LEVEL

THE REFORM OF ADVANCED LEVEL

Michael Kingdon

Head of Research
University of London School Examinations Board

Hodder & Stoughton
LONDON SYDNEY AUCKLAND TORONTO

British Library Cataloguing in Publication Data
Kingdon, Michael
  The reform of advanced level.
  1. England. Secondary schools. G.C.E. (A level) courses
  I. Title
  373.19

  ISBN 0–340–51861–8

First published 1991

Phototypeset by Input Typesetting Ltd, London
Printed in Great Britain for the educational publishing division of
Hodder and Stoughton Ltd, Mill Road, Dunton Green, Sevenoaks,
Kent by St Edmundsbury Press Ltd.

Acknowledgements

The contributions of the following are greatly acknowledged:

Professor Denis Lawton, Chairman of the Consortium for Assessment and Testing in Schools, Chairman of the University of London Schools Examination Board and recently retired Director of the Institute of Education University of London, for his help and encouragement;

Mr Alan Stephenson, The Secretary, University of London School Examinations Board, for his encouragment and for access to the archives of the Board;

Dr Gordon Stobart, Acting Head of Research, University of London School Examinations Boards for his assistance in the development of the initial ideas;

Mr Clive Hart, Assistant Secretary, School Examinations and Assessment Council, for briefing me on current developments;

Mrs Diane Robertson, who typed the original manuscript, and for her patience with my handwriting and frequent changes of mind.

NB The views expressed in this book are those of the author alone and are not to be taken as those of any organisation with which he may be associated.

Contents

Introduction

This book has been written as a contribution to the current debate about the direction in which the General Certificate of Education advanced level system should develop. Almost all those interested in the education of young people agree that significant and immediate change is necessary, and the idea of a broader – and perhaps more vocationally orientated – advanced level curriculum is generally endorsed.

In 1990 the advanced level system was made up of two examinations:

the advanced level (A level) examination introduced in 1951; and

the advanced supplementary level (AS level) examination introduced in 1989.

It is already clear, however, that the introduction of the new AS level examination will not, of itself, significantly broaden the sixth form curriculum as a whole. In both cases the target population is the more academically inclined 18 year old (18+) student, who has studied for two years beyond his/her 16+ examinations (currently the GCSE). The difference between the A and AS level examination is that the second has been designed to make half the demands of the former – half the content and thus half the study time. Nevertheless, the grades awarded are the same and are intended to represent the same depth of study. There is also a third element to the advanced level system – the Special (S) papers. Their purpose is to differentiate the highest levels of attainment, and so are taken voluntarily by the most able students. S papers have their own system of grades.

Today the advanced level system is the subject of new pressures and opportunities. The National Curriculum, now being introduced into schools in England and Wales, seeks to provide a common and broader curriculum for all children aged 5 to 16. When fully

1

implemented it will significantly change the academic makeup of students entering upon advanced level courses. Secondly, the recently introduced General Certificate of Secondary Education (the GCSE) has created other short term problems and long term opportunities. The link between pre- and post-16+ academic courses has been weakened, but some of the features of the GCSE may serve to make the teaching of A level and the planning of future syllabuses easier. The final and most potent force for change is that the political will and the mechanisms for change also exist. The bodies with the greatest direct influence over the examination system – the School Examinations and Assessment Council (SEAC) and the National Curriculum Council (NCC) are seeking to redefine the function of 18+ examinations and to offer students different types of choices.

Today, the General Certificate of Education advanced level system (the GCE A and AS level examinations) represents one step – for most students the most significant step – on the educational ladder that begins in the infant school and which can end with post-graduate and advanced professional education. It is a cause of grave concern to many that only a minority of students in England and Wales reach the A level rung on the ladder and fewer still climb higher. The examination has both summative and predictive functions. It is an assessment of attainment at the end of the sixth form stage of education and the most important element in selection for university entrance.

Part of the problem of the advanced examination system is that it was not, however, originally designed for the purposes that it now serves; instead it has evolved from earlier and simpler systems. No one who today set out to design an examination system from first principles would be likely to create anything as complicated as the advanced level system, with no less than nine competing examination boards and some 390 A level syllabuses (SEAC, 1989a).

The A level examination is highly specialised. Most students take just two or three cognate subjects. This specialism has imposed a narrowness upon the sixth form curriculum, and it is now claimed to be having detrimental effects upon higher education and the commercial life of the nation. Despite its rather eccentric structure and the many criticisms that have been levelled at its specialism, the examination is, nevertheless, held in esteem. For nearly 40 years the A level examination has been accepted by the public in England and Wales as the very embodiment of educational standards. As a result, the many proposals for major structural reform of the examination have usually been treated as semi-sacrilegious.

The processes of A level development continue today and this book is concerned with their direction and rate. Firstly, numerous sets of suggestions have been produced to broaden the GCE A level examination by the radical reform of its structure. Up until now these revolutionary proposals have all been rejected, often because their implementation would have resulted in interference with the standards of the A level examination and may have had profound implications for university and polytechnic degree courses. The 1988 Higginson Report (DES, 1988c) is the most recent example to have been so dismissed.

Secondly, there have been the less radical, and more successful, attempts to broaden the A level examination by supplementing its provision with intermediate examinations. The two most well known, but quite different, examples of this approach are the GCE Alternative Ordinary (AO) level examinations – examined as a separate level between 1976 and 1988 – and the Advanced Supplementary (AS) level examination – which was examined for the first time in 1989. As a result of the introduction of the latter, the combined system of A and AS level examinations is being termed the *advanced level system* and this term will be used throughout this book.

Thirdly, gradual evolutionary changes have been taking place as part of the natural processes of syllabus and examination renewal. These processes have made the GCE A level examination of 1990 very different indeed from the examination introduced nearly 40 years ago. Similar changes are taking place today, with increasing effect.

This book will focus on two main strands of the interwoven pressures for change: firstly, the broadening of the examination and the sixth form curriculum that underlies it; and secondly, the further technical improvement of the examination. The book addresses the fundamental problem of advanced level reform, namely, *the extent to which it is possible to broaden the sixth form curriculum and examinations without diminishing the academic standards of the latter or lengthening higher education courses.* This book, not only discusses the changes that ought to take place to the 18 + examination system, if it is going to fulfil a useful role in the remaining decade of the 20th century and into the 21st, it also discusses how such changes might be encouraged. The implications of advanced level reform are discussed in the context of: the sixth form curriculum; the school examination systems of England, Wales and Northern Ireland; and the underlying issues of syllabus and examination design.

It is hoped that those who teach in tertiary or further education colleges will forgive the author if the term 'sixth form' is used generically to describe the period of education which culminates in formal examinations at 18 or 19 years of age. Similarly, the examination systems of England, Wales, Northern Ireland and some British Commonwealth Countries will be collectively termed the 'English System'. The differing Scottish approach to school examinations precludes reference to a 'British System'.

Chapter 1 sets the scene by describing the A and AS level examinations of 1990 together with their relationship to 16+ examinations and entry to higher education. The role of GCSE examinations, and the alternatives, in the processes of university entrance are discussed. Chapter 2 outlines the origins of the A level examination and especially how it came to be so highly specialist. Chapters 3 and 4 identify and evaluate the forces that have shaped the examination since its introduction in 1951. The former outlines the attempts to broaden the curriculum for students aged 16 to 18 by the introduction of extra subjects into the advanced level examination at 18+, and in some cases into examinations at 17+. The drive towards increased technical efficiency and the development of the examination are reported in the latter.

Chapter 5 concentrates on the one successful attempt, to date, to broaden the A level examination and the sixth form curriculum – the GCE Advanced Supplementary level (the AS level examination). This chapter deals with the features of this new examination. It also considers the practical problems of syllabus design, the implications for schools, and the issues of A and AS level standards. Chapter 6 is devoted to the more recent proposals for change – the Higginson Report published in 1988 is considered in detail and possible reasons for its failure are advanced. The most recent proposals of the SEAC and NCC for the reform of the whole of the 16 to 19 system are also discussed. While the positive reactions of the media and academe to the Higginson Report are not shared – indeed the report is judged to be wanting – it is used to provide a structure for the discussion of the proposed future of the A/AS level system as it has been outlined by SEAC (Chapter 7).

This book ends on a mixed note. It is concluded that the package of AS levels, A levels, learning cores, core skills, cross-curricular themes, transfer of credit with the vocational system proposed by SEAC and undergoing public discussion will broaden the advanced level system. Indeed, the proposals are more integrated than anything seen in the history of the examination and may amount to the establishment of a new entity – an 'English Baccalaureate'? There is no guarantee that standards will be preserved – they will simply be different.

ONE

The GCE advanced level examination system in 1990: perceptions, features and theories

This chapter begins by outlining some of the features of the examination as perceived, firstly, by some of its users and, secondly, by those who work within the GCE system. The former view is based on recent press reports and discussions with members of the public.* The sample for the latter was as typical a mixture of professional people, concerned parents, and former A level students as any other. Nevertheless, no claims are made about the representativeness of their views.

Media reports and the perceptions of my fellow commuters tended to focus on: the role of advanced level examinations in university entrance; its specialism; the age of the students that take the examinations; and, their standards of difficulty. On the basis of their experiences as students, parents and employers, most interviewees were able to describe some of the basic features of the General Certificate of Education advanced level examination. Few, however, had heard of AS levels. They reported:

• that A level examinations are usually taken by school and college students who are 18 years of age (18+) and who have studied for two years beyond the first major school examinations – GCE O level, CSE and GCSE – which in the English school examination system are usually taken at 16+;†

• that A levels can be taken at any age. Many of the people interviewed were able to name relatives or friends who had taken A level examinations in their 20s, 30s or even later. Some were able to quote media reports about very young, or very old students, who had taken A levels and passed with high grades;

• that A levels are more difficult than the examination taken at 16+ so students who have passed the examination are generally considered to be more able. As a result, success at A level examinations offers increased opportunities in employment and improved access to further/higher education;

• that most people take three subjects at A level and 'good grades' in three or two subjects are usually required in order to enter a university, polytechnic and/or some professions. However, good A level results do not guarantee the right to enter higher education; interviews and references are also involved. Conversely, some students succeed in entering higher education without A levels;

• that A level students have considerable choice of subjects. Most A level students will have chosen the majority of the six to nine subjects that they will have taken as part of their 16+ examinations. When preparing for A levels, however, they can – indeed, until recently they are expected to – specialise in a relatively limited area of the curriculum, and this constitutes the major difference between the English and most other western systems of education. Most A level students tend to take groups of two or three related (cognate) subjects but combinations of subjects from different areas of the curriculum are becoming increasingly common;

• that students are able to combine study for the A level examination with study for other academic and/or technical qualification – for example the examinations of the City and Guilds of London Institute (CGLI), the Business and Technician Education Council (BTEC), the Royal Society of Arts (RSA), or the Certificate of PreVocational Education (CPVE) – and this is also becoming more common;

• that only a minority (the exact figures are disputed but certainly less than 20%) of the more able students stay on in full time education to 18 and take the General Certificate of Education advanced level examinations. This is believed to be a far lower proportion than in most other countries in Western Europe or North America;

• that there are a number of GCE advanced level examination boards and that most are associated with universities.

Among the other issues raised by some of the people interviewed and occasional press reports, the following points were made:

• that A levels represent fixed educational standards. Some press reports and interviewees, however, suggested quite the opposite, i.e.

that the standards of the various A level examination boards differed considerably – a charge which will be disputed later in this chapter.

While most people interviewed appeared to be quite content with the GCE A level system, several employers criticised the A level examination claiming:

- that the system was academically (university) dominated;

- that it led to a very narrow curriculum and a lack of intellectual flexibility in the students.

A banker who had worked in Germany and a polytechnic lecturer went on to praise other systems of examination for 18 year olds – The International Baccalaureate, its bigger brother the French Baccalaureate and the German Abitur. None of the interviewees seemed to have any perceptions that the A level examinations system had changed significantly since they had taken them or since it had been introduced in 1951. Most tended to equate their own experiences in working through the A level, or Higher School Certificate, systems with those of current students. When questioned about what advanced level examinations should provide, most stressed university entrance qualifications but also qualities such as maturity and responsibility. Most respondents disliked the idea of new (non-traditional) subjects, although exceptions were made for business studies, computing and perhaps statistics. Conversely, the value of established subjects as the means of developing general skills of numeracy and communication was criticised.

Lastly, in their answers the respondent revealed some of the tensions – even contradictions – that face the advanced level system. None of those interviewed mentioned the S paper system, but when the issue was raised linked it to State Scholarships (which were discontinued after 1962). When the issue of AS level examinations was discussed most interviewees revealed prejudices about the concept of half A levels, wanting both greater breadth and the preservation of traditional A level courses and examinations.

Understanding of the processes by which GCE A level examinations were produced and marked was limited. Perhaps the most positive comments about the advanced level examinations were made by people who were not born in the country. Of those questioned all perceived it as being fair and unbiased.

Having looked at the system from the point of view of the users, what is the more official picture?

The advanced level examination boards in 1990

There are eight GCE examination boards covering England, Wales and Northern Ireland. The English examination boards, with the possible exception of the Associated Examining Board, are strange mixtures of university departments and large international businesses. They enjoy a semi-official status. The six English boards are:

- The Associated Examining Board (AEB)
- The University of Cambridge Local Examinations Syndicate (Cambridge Board)
- The Joint Matriculation Board (JMB)
- The University of London School Examinations Board (London Board)
- The Oxford and Cambridge Schools Examination Board (O&C)
- The Oxford Delegacy of Local Examinations (Oxford Board)

(A seventh board, the Southern Universities' Joint Board (SUJB) closed after the 1990 examination.)

There are also A level examination boards for Wales and Northern Ireland. The first, the Welsh Joint Education Committee (WJEC) is a local education authority organisation; the second, the Northern Ireland Schools Examinations and Assessment Council reports directly to the Northern Ireland Office.

The links between some of the GCE boards are extremely strong. The Cambridge Board, O & C and the SUJB together constitute the COSSEC Consortium and the three boards have recently developed their Advanced Supplementary (AS) level syllabuses in the name of the Consortium. These three boards, together with the East and West Midlands Examination Boards also constitute the Midland Examination Group for GCSE Examinations (MEG). While the AEB and the Oxford Board are competitors at A level, they together make up the Southern Examination Group for GCSE Examinations (SEG). Some formal links exist between the WJEC and the JMB, as do many informal links between the boards in general.

None of the eight GCE examination boards identified above directly receives Government funds, although some do draw monies for non-examination purposes. All eight boards rely on the fees that they receive for the examinations that they conduct. Like any other large businesses they cannot afford to make a loss and competition between them renders it extremely difficult to make a satisfactory surplus. All eight boards are thus in a state of financial and academic competition. None can afford to set their fees too high. Similarly, none can afford to have their syllabuses viewed as out-of-date, uninteresting or of excessively high standard; if they do then they will fail to attract candidates. If their syllabuses are viewed as too easy or superficial, then they risk not being recognised by some universities for entrance purposes and are thus devalued in a different way. It is this combination of the two forms of pressure upon the GCE boards that has lead to the efficiency of the current system as a whole and the wide choice which it now offers to teachers.

While the boards compete with each other for the available candidates, they also co-operate on academic matters. The GCE Secretaries – the senior administrative officers of the boards – meet regularly to discuss matters of mutual interest and to formulate common policies. Meetings of research, computing and administrative staff are also organised on regular bases. These exchanges constitute a major strength of the GCE system.

Oversight of the GCE examination system

The work of the eight GCE boards is currently overseen by the School Examinations and Assessment Council (SEAC) which reports directly to the Department of Education and Science. There is also a branch of SEAC for Wales. The role of SEAC is to approve all syllabuses produced by the boards and to have oversight of their academic standards and procedures. In Northern Ireland assessment responsibilities are all held by NISEAC, and there is a desire to see that the curriculum and examinations of the province do not divert, other than in response to local needs, from the system within England and Wales. SEAC exercises a large measure of centralised control of the 'English' examination system and the advantages and disadvantages of this will be discussed in Chapter 4.

The structure of the GCE boards

Each GCE board brings together three groups of people. Firstly, academics from the universities involved and representatives of teachers organisations together constitute the major committees and formulate policy. In the 1990s it is the latter who hold the majority of seats on the boards' committees and thus may be said to have the greater degree of control and influence. Secondly, the boards contain the professional officers who are responsible for the administration of the examinations. Lastly, there are the Chief Examiners and Assistant Examiners. The former, are responsible for setting examination papers, supervising marking and awarding grades. The latter actually mark the candidates' answer scripts.

The committee members usually give their time freely on behalf of the organisations they represent; the administrators are salaried staff; and, the examiners are paid fees for the work that they do for each examination.

Syllabus development and approval

New syllabuses for individual subjects usually arise because, either as a result of a regular review or perceived problems, it is considered that an existing syllabus needs revision. The reasons for this may be either academic (new thinking about the teaching of the subject or new examination techniques) or commercial (the development of rival syllabuses by other boards and their potential effect on the established candidature). Occasionally, subjects new to the GCE are introduced and syllabuses produced for them. From time to time, there are general initiatives to renew syllabuses. In the first and last cases representatives from all three levels of a board – policy, administration and examinations – meet to discuss the design of the syllabus and its method of assessment.

One of the more contentious issues in syllabus design is the choice of examination components and the weightings (the proportions of final marks) to be allocated to each aspect of the syllabus and examination. New approaches to the teaching of a subject often bring demands for additional assessment techniques, with all of the financial implications that that implies. Draft syllabuses are developed and specimen examination papers produced. This is seldom a quick process; the people involved all have other jobs and duties, and the issues can be complex. There may well be a consultation exercise in which copies of the syllabus and specimen examination papers are circulated to schools and colleges, and the opinion of teachers, plus their approval, are sought. Copies of the syllabus may also be circulated to organisations such as the universities' Standing Council on University Entrance (SCUE), relevant university departments, and associations of teachers of the subject. Finally, when the board is satisfied with the syllabus it is submitted to the SEAC for approval. In the case of completely new subjects the process is similar but there will not, of course, be existing examiners to be consulted.

In the case of AS level syllabuses the processes of development and approval are similar to those of A level. It is only in the consideration of the demands of the AS level syllabuses – teaching and study time – and its intended relationship to A level syllabuses in the same subject, that differences arise. If the examination includes an S paper, this does not usually involve an increase in the syllabus content. Instead, the S paper will seek to assess higher order performances, using the same content.

The teachers are not left to interpret a syllabus on their own. The boards send notes, specimen papers, and reading lists in their routine despatches to schools. Conferences are organised by the boards to discuss new and established syllabuses, and colleges and departments of education throughout the country often do so as well, if the Chief Examiners and boards' staff are available. News and comments about new syllabuses are sometimes reported in the general or specialist educational press.

The development of any new syllabus constitutes a major financial risk for each of the boards. If they introduce too many new features at once teachers may be unwilling to teach it: should they fail to be innovative enough their candidature may drift away to other boards. Some hint of this movement between syllabuses can be identified by inspection of the statistics published annually by each board. Behind the slow trends that this exercise will reveal, are the more dynamic movements as schools experiment with the ever-changing patterns of syllabuses within a subject.

From time to time the responsibility for new syllabuses, and examination, developments has been taken by bodies such as the Nuffield Foundation, the Schools Council, subject teachers organisations, or even colleges of higher education (see Chapter 4). The intention of these curriculum development projects has usually been to influence the teaching of a subject as a whole. Special examinations have often been devised to assess them and these have usually been examined by one GCE board on behalf of the others. The Nuffield Science Teaching Project, the School Mathematics Project, Mathematics in Education and Industry Project, the Schools Classic Project (Latin) and Schools Council Geography are probably the most well known examples. However, as will be indicated in later chapters, there are some doubts about the future of this approach to syllabus and examination development.

The appointment and training of examiners

By far the largest number of people involved in the examination process are the Assistant Examiners whose job it is, under the direction of the Chief or Senior Examiners, to mark the examination papers. Advertisements for Assistant Examiners appear regularly on staff room notice boards and those with suitable qualifications and teaching experience are invited to apply. Almost all boards provide regular training courses for their Assistant Examiners.

The key people in the examination process are the Chief or Senior Examiners, who are not only responsible for the setting of examination papers and for the organisation of their marking, they usually play a key role in the development of syllabuses. There is some competition between the boards to appoint the best Chief Examiners, who must be viewed as leaders in the current thinking about the teaching of their subjects. Many Chief Examiners are drawn from the ranks of the Assistant Examiners who have marked papers in previous years, but this is not essential.

The remaining group of examiners are the Assistant Chief Examiners who are intermediate in status between the Assistants and Chiefs. Assistant Chiefs are responsible for overseeing the marking of teams of Assistant Examiners, especially the new ones if the numbers of Assistant Examiners are too large for the Chief Examiners to supervise directly. Consequently only the more popular subjects tend to have Assistant Chiefs.

Setting examination papers

The main GCE advanced level examinations take place in June. However, many of the boards also organise examinations in November or January, depending on their tradition. Entries are open to all, but these examinations are usually associated, in many people's minds, with candidates resitting subjects. There are also significant numbers of candidates who take one (but not usually more) of their A levels early in order to relieve some of the pressures upon them in the following June. Finally, the winter examinations are of a greater importance overseas as they correspond better with the usual academic year in the Southern hemisphere. Increasing financial pressures are tending to restrict the winter examinations to core subjects only and the future of this arrangement as a whole may be in doubt. Whether it is a summer or a winter examination that is being written, the processes and the standards are the same.

For the schools, the cycle of an advanced level examination begins when the syllabuses are distributed to schools, some two to three years before the candidates sit the corresponding examination papers.

Not long after the syllabuses are in the schools and colleges, the Chief Examiners meet to plan the writing of the papers. Nowadays few A level examinations have as small a number as two examination papers, the more common numbers being 3, 4 or 5. Exceptionally, an A level may be made up of 6, 7 or even 8 components. AS level examinations have fewer components, but usually half or more than the corresponding A level. A and AS levels frequently share components or sections.

The practice in most GCE boards is to appoint one Chief Examiner for each written paper and special arrangements are made for other examination components such as teachers' assessments, multiple choice questions, fieldwork, orals and practicals. Each Chief Examiner drafts his or her paper(s) and then they meet as a team, under the chairmanship of a Moderator or Senior Chief Examiner, to review (moderate) each others' papers. The purpose of this process is to ensure the fairness of the examination papers as a whole and it is also the point at which the marking schemes for the papers are developed and approved. Each advanced level examination must provide an adequate sampling of the syllabus, must not be more or less difficult than the previous examinations and must be free of gender, cultural or regional biases. Many boards also have a system of consulting teacher moderators for their views. Some parts of the examination, e.g. multiple choice questions and practical tests, may have been tried out in formal and informal trials.

When the review process has been completed and the papers finalised they are then sent for printing. As the examination papers pass through the printing stages the officers of the board, together with the Chief Examiners, have responsibility for proof-reading and the production of the necessary illustrations. No board can afford to have a reputation for sloppy presentation and errata are kept to the lowest possible number.

Entries for the examination

Entries for the examination are accepted some months in advance: January/February for the June examination, September for the autumn/winter. Typically there are three groups of candidates of whom the first constitute by far the largest number: school candidates – of whom a small number may be students who have left that particular school but are returning to re-sit examinations; private candidates who enter via a school or college, or directly through the boards; and, overseas candidates. Each entry has to be accompanied by the appropriate fee, and in the maintained schools in England and Wales these are usually paid for by the Local Education Authorities. Private candidates have to pay their own fees and a variety of arrangements are used for overseas candidates.

In 1990 the total number of candidates entering for the advanced level examination was approximately 300 000, and between them they made over 600 000 subject entries. These numbers can only be approximate: many candidates entered for the advanced level examinations of different boards and one or two may even have attempted double entries. When it is also remembered that some may be re-sitting the examinations, perhaps not for the first time, it is difficult to estimate the total proportion of students in any school year that sit and pass advanced level examinations.

Administration of the advanced level examination

Once the entries have been received, the examination boards have to make the links between the student, the examination papers that he or she will sit, and Assistant Examiners who mark the papers. Each student is issued with a timetable indicating the time, place and duration of the examination papers and the appropriate numbers of papers have to be despatched to the examination centres, usually a school or college, in advance. Special arrangements have to be made for the non-written paper examination components – teacher assessed work, practical and oral examinations.

Teachers are asked to make initial assessments – teachers' assessments (TA) – of those elements of the advanced level examination which have been undertaken over time and/or are not easy transportable to the board. Projects and field work may be examples of the first, and cookery and various forms of art work examples of the second. Two processes are commonly used to try to ensure that the TA marks that come from different schools and colleges are comparable. The first is *pre-assessment standardisation*. The board issues clear instructions, assessment criteria and possibly even pre-marked samples of work to help the teachers to make the initial assessments. In some cases training for the teachers is also provided, and in exceptional cases the maintenance of a satisfactory standard of assessment may be a condition for continued participation with a particular syllabus.

The second technique is *post-assessment moderation*. Samples of the work assessed by the teacher are re-marked by a moderator apponted by the board. This may be achieved either by visits to the school or the submission of samples. In a limited number of cases statistical moderation is applied. The teachers' assessments are adjusted to come into line with the same candidates' performances on some other aspect(s) of the examination. Statistical moderation of this form tends to be very unpopular with the teachers and, in the author's view, cannot be fully justified on statistical or logical grounds.

The teacher assessed components of a GCE advanced level examination represent the one area in which the student is not treated completely as an individual. His or her final marks must depend to a small extent upon the performance of the school or teaching group to which he or she belonged. This problem is acknowledged by all involved and it is generally accepted that the increased validity which results from the use of teacher assessment is more than justified by the small compromises to reliability that have to be made. (The meanings of these technical terms and an explanation of the relationships between them are outlined later in this chapter.)

Practical examinations are usually organised before the written papers are taken. Practicals demand a high degree of involvement by the school or college in their preparation. Instructions have to be issued by the examination boards to the teachers concerned who have to prepare the necessary materials. The practical examinations may be marked either by the submission of the results to the examination board or by teacher assessment.

Oral examinations are usually conducted by visiting examiners.

Most examination boards spend a disproportionate amount of their resources on the training of oral examiners, arranging their visits and standardising their marking in the attempt to ensure overall fairness. Once again, this effort is necessitated by the need to ensure adequate validity and reliability. Oral examining is usually applied in modern languages. Its use with languages other than the main five – French, German, Spanish, Italian and Russian – is less frequent, due to the problems of finding suitable examiners. Oral examinations are also used sometimes in association with project and practical work in other areas of the curriculum, and this tendency is increasing.

The arrangements for the conduct of the written paper examinations are now traditional. Each candidate sits at a small table in a large room, with aisles on either side, and with the tables sufficiently far apart for copying to be impossible. During the examination, which is very carefully timed, invigilators patrol, making sure that all rules of the examination are strictly adhered to. At the end of the examination the papers are collected and despatched to Assistant Examiners who mark the papers, usually at home.

Finally, special arrangements may have to be made for candidates who suffer from particular forms of disadvantage or disability: tactile diagrams may be provided for blind candidates; extra time for dyslexic candidates; amanuenses for those with manipulatory difficulties. In the cases of those candidates who, through temporary or permanent illnesses or disability, may be unable to attend the examination room, the boards appoint visiting invigilators to supervise the conduct of the examination in the candidate's home.

The examination timetables for the major subjects are agreed between the boards but there are occasional clashes. These are becoming increasingly common as a result of both pressure on the examination period due to the larger number of examination components and the tendency of more students to study cross-curricular and cross-board combinations of subjects. The problems and the solutions tend to be individual and every attempt is made to be fair to students and their circumstances. When problems cannot easily be resolved by rescheduling papers or providing alternatives, it may be necessary for candidates to be chaperoned between one examination paper and the next. In extreme cases, it is not unknown for examination candidates to spend the night at the home of one of the members of staff of their school or college.

The marking of examination papers

Once the Assistant Examiners have passed the training course, they are appointed to a panel of examiners. When the entries for an examination subject are known the board's officers then invite the

(c) *Comparability between boards.* The advanced level grades awarded must be comparable with the grades awarded by other GCE boards' syllabuses for the same subject at the same level.

(d) *Comparability between subjects.* The advanced level grades awarded in any one subject need to be comparable with the grades awarded for other subjects examined by the same board.

All four forms of comparability apply separately to A and AS level examinations. The first form of comparability – over time – is usually ensured by the consideration of qualitative information from the current and previous examinations. Candidates' scripts, the marking schemes, the examination papers and comments about previous examinations, are all compared. Quantitative analyses also have a function in questioning or confirming the judgement of the Chief Examiners. The second form of comparability – between syllabuses – is usually achieved by ensuring that there is some commonality in the people involved in the award of each syllabuses. Again the basis of judgement is the comparison of the qualitative information identified above. If one or more syllabuses contain a common paper (or papers) these may be used as a guide – although not a particularly binding one – to the relative difficulty of the individual syllabuses.

The third form of comparability – between GCE boards – has exercised the research officers of the boards for the past 25 years or so. A large number of studies have been conducted to try and identify any board whose syllabus is different from those of the other boards. Indeed, a whole literature of studies has been developed (e.g. Bardell *et al.*, 1978; Forrest and Shoesmith, 1985) but very few examples of 'incomparability' have been identified. Any consideration of differences between the GCE boards – whether on a qualitative or a quantitative basis – have to be conducted after each board has made its initial awards and the results have been published (see Chapter 4).

The assessment of comparability between different subjects (d) also tends to be a post-examination activity and often has to be conducted in statistical terms. Despite the qualitative differences between subjects many people concerned with the A level examinations – university admissions tutors, teachers and parents – expect the examination grades in one subject to represent the same level of demand on students as those in another subject. Indeed the Universities' Central Council on Admissions (UCCA) which administers the processes of application for university places, operates a system in which A and AS level grades are converted to numerical points. The confirmation of a student's entry into university often depends very largely upon the number of points that they have been able to accumulate in the GCE advanced level examination. The GCE boards, therefore, use a variety of procedures to try to identify instances of apparent incomparability. The most common is the use of 'subject pairs' analyses (Forrest and Vickerman, 1982). As with the results of the inter-board comparability studies, any corrective action that has to be taken is applied in future examinations.

The introduction of AS levels in 1989 created the need for a fifth form of comparability – the comparability of demands between A and AS level examinations. Where there are common papers or sections between A and AS levels these are expected to be used as the basis of judgement. The approach adopted for this problem of comparability is similar to that used for the second form – common examiners. (We will return to this issue in Chapter 5.)

Under arrangements agreed between the Department of Education and Science, the Secondary Examinations Council (the immediate forerunner of the present SEAC) and the GCE boards in 1987, A level grades are awarded on a seven point scale. When AS levels were introduced in 1989 the same system was used but, in theory and in practice, AS level grades have exactly half the value of the corresponding A level grades. The highest grade in each case is grade A, which for A level counts ten points in the UCCA system and for AS level, five. The lowest grade of pass is grade E, which counts two and one point respectively. Below grade E there is a grade N indicating a 'near-miss' and finally at the lowest end of the quality range a grade U indicating an unclassified result. Grades E, B and A are awarded on the basis of the qualities inherent in the candidates' answer papers.

During the advanced level awards the Chief Examiners, acting as a team, look at large samples of candidates' answers and decide which marks for each paper (or in the case of some boards, the subject as a whole) they will accept as the lowest level of performance compatible with the award of grades E, B and A. Grades C and D are determined for the subject as a whole by dividing the mark range from the lowest mark of grade B to the lowest mark of grade E into three equal divisions (see Table 1 for a worked example). Grade N is determined by an extension of this process.

Fixing the grades – a hypothetical example

If during the award of an A level subject grade E, B and A were to be set at, say, 40%, 64% and 71% there would be 24 marks between the minimum mark of grade E and the minimum mark of grade B. As a result, grade C would be set at 56 marks, grade D at 48 marks and grade N at 32 marks. This means that the mark range for each of these grades would be the same, i.e. eight marks. If the mark range for the minimum mark of grade E to grade B is not easily divisible by three, there are agreed policies about what to do.

S paper grades are awarded on a different system of grades: 1

19

Table 1 *Awarding advanced level grades: an example*

percentage marks	grade	notes
71% and above	A	fixed by quality of work
64% to 70% (mark range = 8%)	B	fixed by quality of work
56% to 63% (mark range = 8%)	C	fixed using mark range
48% to 55% (mark range = 8%)	D	fixed using mark range
40% to 47% (mark range = 8%)	E	fixed by quality of work
32% to 39%	N	fixed using mark range
0% to 31%	U	

total mark range low B to low E = 24%

(distinction); 2 (merit); and U (unclassified). The grades are awarded entirely on the basis of the quality of work, but grades 1 and 2 cannot be awarded to a candidate unless he or she has been awarded an A level pass grade for the same syllabus, in the same examination. Comparability between S paper grades in different subjects is seldom an issue. Few candidates sit more than one S paper and the meanings of grades are deeply embedded within the subjects.

Once provisional grade boundaries have been determined using assessments of the quality of the candidates' work, a number of statistical techniques are used to question or confirm the Chief Examiners' judgements. If grades are awarded by component it is necessary, when the grade points of the subject as a whole are determined, to make allowances for the bunching of marks (regression) which inevitably occurs when less than perfectly correlated marks are combined. All candidates whose marks are on or above the final grade points are awarded those grades. Those candidates whose final marks as a whole, or for some individual papers, fall just below these grade points are then subjected to a process termed *borderlining*.

Almost all boards use a borderlining procedure. This involves Chief Examiners reviewing the answer scripts of candidates who have just failed to achieve a particular advanced level grade. They may look for instances where an Assistant Examiner has failed to give sufficient credit for correct answers or where the answers as a whole appear to be worth more than the mark scheme has allowed. Where such instances are found the candidates may be given extra credit and this sometimes results in the award of the higher grade.

Special arrangements are made for all those candidates, who through no fault of their own, are disadvantaged during the examination period and whose performance is therefore diminished. The GCE boards make a distinction between, firstly, those candidates who completed all of the examination papers in a subject but whose performance might have been reduced by illness or accident, and, secondly, those candidates who missed some of the examination papers. In both cases the procedure begins with the school or college reporting the matter to the examination board. Using pre-issued forms, the teachers in the school or college prepare a report about the problem, attaching any medical certificates or other evidence. They supply information about the affected candidate's abilities with respect to other candidates in the same centre that have taken the same examination papers. All of the disadvantaged candidates are then given individual consideration by Chief Examiners and/or board officers. In the case of the first group of candidates additional marks may be awarded, the number depending upon the nature of the extenuating circumstances. In the second case, estimates have to be made about a candidate's performance on the paper (or papers) that they did not sit or complete: such awards are termed aegrotat awards.

The publication of results and appeals

Once the grades have been awarded for the individual subjects the complete advanced level results for that board are assembled for each candidate. Provisional results slips are printed by the boards' computers and issued to each school. All of the boards use a process of embargoed mailing: the results are put into the post some days before the official publication date and the Post Office delivers them on the agreed day. The results slips for individual candidates are then distributed by the schools themselves.

Following the publication of the provisional results, the schools may make appeals on behalf of individual candidates and in exceptional cases whole classes. When a candidate has failed to achieve the expected grade the school may request several types of checks upon the result. These may vary from, a purely clerical check to see that the marks have been accurately added up, transcribed from the individual papers and that the grade has been correctly calculated, to a complete remark of the candidate's answers and the preparation of a full report about his or her performance. When such an appeal results in a change of grade for the candidate, checks are also applied to a selection of the other candidates' work marked by the same Assistant Examiner(s) and/or candidates who have entered through the same school. Once the necessary appeals have been resolved and the results finalised, certificates are issued.

Post award activities

The publication of results, the appeals and the issue of certificates are not the end of the cycle. Reports are prepared by its Chief Examiners on the examination of each syllabus and these are presented to the boards' committees and may be issued to schools. Other reports are produced by groups outside the boards. The teachers' comments are collated by their unions, working together through standing joint committees, and submitted to the boards who prepare responses. SEAC also conducts scrutinies of selected examinations. Each board prepares award statistics, and undertakes internal reviews and analyses. Together the boards produce comparisons of their work, and these may incorporate comparability studies. The object of all of this work is to ensure the efficiency and fairness of the GCE examination. Lastly, conferences with the teachers may be organised to update them on the features of the syllabuses and examinations.

The cycle of the examination

From the commissioning of papers to the completion of any post-examination inter-board studies may involve a three year cycle. If the post-examination studies reveal that major changes are necessary to the syllabus and/or the scheme of examination, corrective action may take several years to implement. Minor revisions can be dealt with in time for the next year's examination by circulars sent to the schools and teachers.

The cycle, of conducting examinations, evaluating them, improving them and conducting them again, has been one of the most powerful forces that has led to the improvement of the advanced level examination system. The examinations are now acknowledged to be of high academic standard, and their administration to be as fair as possible to all candidates. While the administration is not above criticism, it has served as a model for the development of many other systems of public examination worldwide. The development of the administrative system has been an important part of the history of the examination and developments continue today.

The role of A and AS level in the process of admission to higher education

Even when a student has gained good A level (and possibly AS level) grades this does not guarantee admission to higher education courses.

In the system in use in the UK it is necessary for students to make personal applications to a limited number of institutions of higher education. In the case of the universities this is the Universities Central Council on Admissions (UCCA) and for polytechnics the Polytechnics Council for the Admission of Students (PCAS). (The reason that may lead an individual student to choose particular university or polytechnic courses is not relevant here.) Each department or faculty of a university or polytechnic will have its own clearly stated advanced level entry requirements.

While it is possible to enter higher education with just two A level passes at the lowest grades (or an equivalent combination of A and/or AS level), significantly higher grades are usually necessary. Indeed, for many university faculties three or more A grade passes at A level are not unheard of, and S paper passes are sometimes required. When students apply for higher education courses they have usually not sat their advanced level examinations and this is one of the reasons why the references from their schools and colleges are important. One of the functions of the reference supplied is to offer a prediction of performance in forthcoming advanced level examinations. A second, and in many cases equally important, function is to indicate something about the student as a person.

While success in the academic aspects of the sixth form is essential, the student is expected to be something more than a mere swot. The universities in particular look not only for somebody who is academically able but somebody who is also 'rounded'. The criteria for this latter quality are somewhat ill defined. Those students who have held a position in a school or community society, who have undertaken expeditions, who have interesting hobbies, who are to be successful in an artistic or a sporting line, are all taken as being 'rounded'. The reasons for such a necessity are partly traditional and partly social. In pre-A level days, evidence that a student came from the 'right sort' of school, family, or social class was seen as important. In more recent times involvement in non-academic fields is taken as a sign of maturity. Additionally, it must be remembered that universities are a community in which staff and students work closely together for some years. Breadth of experience may thus make for more interesting interchanges between staff and students and may also serve to enhance post-graduate employment prospects. The most important issue here is that qualities, not assessed by advanced level examinations, are usually required in addition to academic achievements.

Once an application is made, most institutes of higher education interview the students before they decide upon those students to whom they might offer conditional places. While these interviews tend to focus upon academic matters, the personal characteristics of the student – their ability to communicate, how presentable they are

23

rather than detailed analyses, then it is the *face validity* which is being assessed.

Construct validity – the degree to which an advanced level examination assesses a related body of skills and content.

Predictive validity – the degree to which the advanced level examination can predict performance in other stages of the education process, employment and/or life.

The assessment of content and face validity is essentially judgmental. Construct and predictability validity can be quantified but, as neither is entirely appropriate to the advanced level situation this is not often attempted. The measurement of construct validity is sometimes undertaken for individual components such as multiple choice papers, but as an A or AS level examination as a whole tends to encompass many diverse skills and areas of content, this can seldom be meaningfully attempted for a complete examination. The assessment of predictive validity has sometimes been attempted for A level examinations with unsatisfactory results. Comparisons can be made between advanced level grades and degree results but as only the better advanced level candidates enter university there are serious problems of restricted scales of measurement.

The reliability of an examination is a measure of its consistency. Indices of reliability – test/retest, split half etc. and other measures of inherent reliability – are commonly used for many types of psychometric tests, but again not for advanced level examinations as a whole. Very few of the statistical measures of reliability are completely appropriate due to the complexity of the GCE examination. Indices tend only to be used in the case of multiple choice questions, could be applied to short answer and other objective questions, but are seldom used for other forms of advanced level assessment.

It is quite possible for an examination to be thoroughly reliable but invalid. It is not possible, however, for the validity of an examination to exceed its reliability. Therefore, the hope is that advanced level examinations will be as reliable as they can be, and as valid as that measure of reliability permits.

Early in the history of the A level examination, (see Chapters 2 and 4), there were concerns about the reliability of the examination and objective testing techniques were introduced partly to resolve this problem and partly in response to other (curricular) initiatives. Since that time greater emphasis has been placed on trying to increase the validity of the examination but with as little sacrifice to its reliability as possible. In the introduction to the GCSE National Criteria, one of the aims of that examination is stated as 'making the important assessable rather than making the assessable important'. While the thrust towards increased validity has tended to take place more at 18+ than at 16+, the movement has yet to be codified and enshrined in the same way. Unfortunately, the slow and positive technical developments that have taken place at 18+ have tended to go unnoticed by those who work outside the advanced level system.

Coherence: A and AS level as subject examinations

The coherence of an advanced level examination stems from the degree to which the syllabus and examinations sample a subject in a clear and organised way.

Since their earliest beginnings, 18+ examinations for school examinations have been based on subjects. But what precisely is a subject? King and Brownell (1966) have identified an academic subject as being a 'community of discourse', or expressed another way, a group of like-minded scholars. From the very earliest times scholars have sub-divided knowledge and have tended to specialise in an area (or areas) of academic endeavour. Within groups interested in similar intellectual areas there developed consensuses about the topics that were worthy of investigation and how such topics should be investigated. Further similar types of problems were found over time to require similar methodologies. Subjects are therefore partly epistemological and partly social phenomena.

Since education in European universities took its present form academic study has been organised along subject lines. Even by the time the University of London was founded and its first matriculation examinations established, it was probably unthinkable to the academics involved that their teaching and examinations would be based in any other way. The predecessors of the A level examination (see Chapter 2) have inherited these attitudes. More recently in the period between the agreement in 1985 to establish the new AS level examination and the first examination in 1989, the syllabuses were again developed along the same lines. At advanced level the syllabuses tend to contain traditional ideas, skills and knowledge that have proved useful in the past and will hopefully do so in the future. A and AS level examinations also try to provide both a flavour of study at higher level and the foundations for such later study, all as well as being a coherent sampling of the subject in their own right. There is thus an element of discipleship inherent in the study of advanced level subjects, although the degree to which it has been emphasised has varied over time.

In many ways subjects are equally important within the schools and colleges that prepare advanced level students. Such institutions are organised along subject lines. They have hierarchies both between and within the subjects, and subjects are one of the ways in which identity and status is conferred on members of the teaching staff, e.g. 'she's the head of maths', 'he teaches economics'. Attempts in the past to broaden the sixth form curriculum by forging cross-subject links, have been largely unsuccessful partly because of these attitudes. Even where teachers, and sometimes universities, have been in support of such developments, they have not tended to prove popular with parents and students.

The attitude that academic excellence is enshrined within established subjects has led to problems when new subjects have appeared. Perhaps because of negative attitudes to cross-curricular study, new subjects have often had to win a battle for acceptance. The rise of statistics, computing and environmental studies are recent examples. For the first two acceptance was easier – they were sub-divisions of other high status subjects and had immediate appeal. Study within these two areas was not only of value in its own right but supportive of work in other school subjects. Environmental studies had a more difficult start. As a new, and a hybrid, subject it had to prove its difference from the existing areas of study from which it had arisen. All new subjects risk being seen as 'soft options' and have tended to respond to this danger by producing very elaborate (and expensive) schemes of examination.

One of the unfortunate aspects of the tradition of organising the study and examination of academic pupils at 18+ along subject lines, has been a bias against vocational work. It is only recently that the vocational implications of subjects have been seen as valuable. With this growing attitude it may well be possible now to contemplate the organisation of, at least part, of the advanced level system along other than academic subject lines.

Research over the past 15 years or so into school examinations at 16+ and 18+ has tended to reinforce the subject model. As syllabuses have developed and have come to assess new areas of skill and content, new examination techniques have had to be developed. Once again it is the curricular pressures that have led, and assessment that has followed. Nevertheless, it is the expectation of all concerned with the advanced level examinations that all of the questions, and all of the papers should be shown to be measuring a coherent area of academic interest.

The technique used to assess the coherence has been correlation analysis.* Parts of questions, questions within the same paper and the papers that make up an examination should, it is reasoned, all be positively and significantly correlated with each other: this is taken as evidence that they are measuring related things. The magnitude of the correlation coefficients involved can vary quite considerably

---

* At a simple level, the correlation coefficient (r) is a measure of the degree to which two sets of students' marks indicate similar rank orders. If $r = +1$ the two mark orders are the same, if $r = -1$ they are exactly reversed and if $r = 0$ there is no connection between the two sets of marks. Depending upon the number of students involved, near zero correlation coefficients may not be significant in either statistical or educational terms.

from subject to subject, and indeed from paper to paper. Should any correlation analysis reveal near zero correlation coefficients, between elements of the examination, this would be taken as evidence of distinct dimensions of performance within the same subject and possible evidence of a lack of coherence.

One problem about the correlational integrity of advanced level examinations has arisen in parallel with the syllabus changes over the past 20 years or so. As new areas of content and skill have been introduced, new components have been developed to assess them. The inclusion of new examination components in an existing A level subject causes some problems. A case has to be made that the new component is needed to assess features of the subject not already assessed by existing components. (The number of examination components has obvious financial and other resource implications.) If, on the one hand, the correlations between the new component and the established ones are high, this is taken to indicate that there is already considerable academic overlap in what is assessed. If correlation is too low, on the other hand, this would be taken as evidence that the new component is assessing something that lies outside the area of the established examination. Even if the correlation between the new components and the established ones is low, positive but still significant, there are still problems. One of the most fundamental statistical problems facing advanced level syllabus and examination designers is that of regression. It is an inevitable statistical fact that, as sets of less than perfectly correlated marks are combined together, there is a tendency for the marks to bunch around the mean. When the inter-correlations between the individual sets of marks are low – as tends to be the case for new examination components – then this bunching effect is all the greater. As will be explained below, low correlations and the associated regression (bunching of marks) leads to one of the problems facing the English school examination system, that of poor discrimination.

Norm- and criterion-referenced assessment

The A level examination has often been criticised as being a norm-referenced examination, i.e. it is suggested that the process of awarding A level grades is essentially a statistical one. Some features of the previous and current system of awarding A level grades (see Chapter 4) tend to reinforce this unfortunate perception. The alternative to a norm-referenced examination would be one based upon a student demonstrating his or her mastery of defined skills, concepts and knowledge. This is called a criterion-referenced system of assessment.

In practice, A and AS level examinations exist somewhere in the middle of the continuum that stretches from norm referencing at one extreme to criterion referencing at the other. Those that work in the examination system are able to place the different GCE boards at points on this continuum. These differences, are a cause of concern to the SEAC and the subject of much discussion between the boards. However, the differences are seldom large enough to have shown up in the inter-board comparability studies.

There are many pressures upon the A level examination at the present time which are tending to move it in the direction of criterion referencing. While there appear to be many advantages that might result from such a movement, the warning must be sounded about achieving a fully criterion-referenced system. Some features of advanced level examinations, such as comparability between subjects, would become meaningless if this were to occur. Orr and Nuttall (1983) and Kingdon and Stobart (1988) have both cited some of the problems that would follow the development of a fully criterion-referenced system at 16+. For the foreseeable future the GCE A and AS level examinations will continue to be a blend of norm- and criterion-referenced assessment.

The discrimination and differentiation of advanced level examinations

Discrimination is a somewhat dated term. It is used here in a technical sense to mean that property of the examination which ensures that the individual A and AS level grades have meaning.

Until comparatively recently the efficiency of an A level examination has tended to be assessed in terms of statistical properties of the distribution of candidates' marks, the mean mark and the standard deviation. If the average mark for each paper or the examination as a whole was about 50% it was assumed that the examiners had estimated the ability of the candidature accurately. To award grades successfully, it was also important to make sure that there was a good spread in the marks and this was evidenced by the standard deviation. If the standard deviation was high the examination was deemed to be efficient and grades could, in turn, be differentiated by wider mark ranges. If the standard deviation was low then this would indicate either that the candidature was more homogeneous than usual or that the examination as a whole had failed to spread the marks sufficiently. Such cases lead to difficulty in awarding grades.

The current system of awarding grades introduced in 1987 was a response to what was seen as poor discrimination in the system as a whole but especially in the area of grade C (see Whittaker and Forrest, 1983). One of the disadvantages inherent in both 16+ and 18+ examinations in defining the discrimination of examinations in statistical terms is that it has always been very difficult to decide exactly what it is that candidates have actually done to earn their grades. Less able candidates tended to gain their low grades as a result of failing to gain sufficient marks to be awarded a higher grade. When analyses were undertaken to see what they had achieved, it was often revealed that their general performance in the examination lacked coherence and was characterised by the gaining of a few marks here and a few marks there. Even at the higher end of the ability range it has often been very difficult to see how, in qualitative terms, the more able candidates had achieved their better results. When performance at one grade was compared with that immediately above or below then the problem became even greater.

Partly as a response to the problem of coherence, partly in an attempt to increase the discrimination of individual examination papers, and partly as a result of a desire to increase the accountability of the examination, discrimination has tended to become defined more in terms of qualities. As part of this process, the efforts to improve the quality of the advanced level examination has turned from statistical properties of examinations to features of the syllabuses themselves and the term discrimination has given way to the concept of differentiation. One of the solutions to the problem of assessing a wide range of ability at in the GCSE has been the introduction of strategies – different forms of differentiation – to enable all students to achieve at their own level. Examples include: differentiated combinations of papers for the more and less able students; questions that differentiate by outcome; structured questions that increase in difficulty as a student proceeds through the different parts. A further aspect of this process is the increasing emphasis on positive achievement. This idea was developed in the GCSE examination and focuses on assessing what a student can do, rather than what he or she cannot. The concepts of differentiation and positive achievement are now coming to be applied to advanced level examinations but few current syllabuses were designed with them in mind.

Summative assessment

Advanced level examinations are often considered to be hurdles on the path that leads from school or college to higher education. More importantly, they have a summative role. They are assessments of attainment at the end of an important stage of education. Although advanced level results may contribute to a student's educational achievement, they do not have a formative role *per se*. Even formal assessments made by teachers, are usually not revealed to the students, and are combined with other examination marks during the award of the overall subject grade.

31

Some changes are taking place in the way advanced level results are reported. Some boards are now providing unofficial profiles of students' results in different examination components, but the practice is not widespread. Trials of modular syllabuses, which use end-of-module assessment as a supplement or alternative to the usual summative examination, have taken place recently. Even here, however, the results of the end of module assessments are not revealed to students. (See page 107.) Advanced level examinations in 1990, therefore, remain mostly summative in nature.

GCE examinations in 1990

The very complicated set of inter-connecting procedures that make up the advanced level examination cycles were not put into place overnight. Like so much of English society, the school examination system is riven with precedents. Each facet of the system has arisen as the result of requests, problems or opportunities that have occurred over time. They, in some cases, need only to have happened once for changes to be made to the procedures underlying the examination and for them instantly to become part of the established fabric of the examination. Many of the procedures described above have their origins in the middle of the last century. As a result, today's advanced level examinations carry with them a hidden and unusually unstated tradition. In the next few chapters we will explore how, and why, current advanced level examinations have come to have their current complex form.

1990 also saw the advanced level examinations in a state of technical transition. They are becoming increasingly criterion-referenced and associated with this is greater emphasis on validity and positive assessment. The examinations are also subject to increasing pressures and are being constrained by the tensions between:

(a) developments taking place lower down the school curriculum, and the demands of (and apparent inertia of much of) higher education;

(b) increasing financial pressures, and tighter central controls.

TWO

Advanced level origins

Nineteenth-century matriculation examinations

There are two examinations which can be identified as the progenitors of the General Certificate of Education advanced level system. The claim for the first – the University of London matriculation examination, introduced in 1838 – is based on its link with university entrance and to the foundation of English examination systems in general. The claim for the second – the same university's intermediate examination, introduced in 1851 – is based on its link with current 18+ examinations.

In the early 19th century the only English institutions of higher education that offered fully recognised degree qualifications were the universities of Oxford and Cambridge. Both were tied closely to the upper and professional classes, and to the Church of England. Oxford and Cambridge drew their students from the developing 'public' school system and both used similar systems of admission. Schemes of competitive exhibitions and scholarships did exist, but for those students with means, the process was more socially than academically selective – a letter from a public school house master was often sufficient. Students formally became undergraduates when their names were entered on the 'matricula' or list of recognised students.

It was the creation of the University of London that led to the development of the first public – used here in the general rather than the selective meaning of the word – university examinations. A major factor in the foundation of the University of London was the desire of the rising middle class to establish a system of higher education that was free of the privilege inherent in the Oxbridge systems. For many years after its foundation in 1836 the University provided the only viable alternative to the Oxbridge route to higher education and certain professions.

The development of examinations for school students during most of the 19th century is inextricably linked with the spread of the

University of London degree and pre-degree examinations throughout Britain and the developing British Empire. Gradually other universities, or groups of universities, established examination-based systems of matriculation and other school examinations. Some of these universities had their origins as colleges that had entered students for the London matriculation and degree examinations. They, in turn, adopted the London procedures with which they had become familiar.

How did one university come to have such an influence on the system of school examinations? What were the examinations like and what were their effects upon the schools of the day?

The development of the University of London Matriculation Examination – the first general school examination

The mid-1830s saw two 'universities' in London. The first, which became University College London had been founded in 1829 and the second King's College in 1832; neither had the power to grant degrees. In 1836, an act of Parliament established a third body, the University of London, to conduct examinations but not to teach students. This new university was, in effect, the first examination board. University and King's Colleges became the first two colleges of the University of London.

Almost as soon as the Senate of the new university began work in January 1837, it considered 'under what circumstances students might be admitted to degree courses'. An entrance or matriculation examination was established which all prospective students had to pass at least two years before taking their Bachelor of Arts Degree. It was therefore possible, but very unusual, for a student to graduate at 18. Success in the BA degree gave in turn admission to first degrees in the University's other two faculties, medicine and law, and to higher degrees in arts.

The *raison d'être* for the establishment of the University of London was the avoidance of the privilege inherent in the contemporary Oxbridge systems. Its examinations had therefore to be fair, and be seen to be fair. As a result the new university conducted its matriculation and other examinations entirely by written papers – a concept that seems to be deeply embedded in the British psyche to this day.

The first matriculation examination took place in the week that began on 5 November 1838, just over 150 years ago. All of the candidates, only 23 in number, were from University and King's Colleges. There were six compulsory subjects. Entrance to the matriculation examination was open to anyone who was over the age of 16 and who paid the fee of £2. In the following two weeks there were a further twelve papers for candidates who wished to compete for the Honours Examinations that led to the award of university exhibitions of £30 for the two years of the BA course.

The subjects examined in the matriculation and Honours Examinations were:

Matriculation
mathematics – arithmetic and algebra
English history
Greek – classic and history
chemistry or natural history (botany)
mathematics – algebra and geometry
Roman – classic and history

Honours: mathematics/natural philosophy
arithmetic, algebra and geometry
trigonometry and conic sections
mechanics
problems of natural philosophy
hydrostatics and dynamics
problems in pure mathematics

Honours: classics
Greek (two papers)
Latin – prose composition
Latin translation (two papers)
English composition

This first matriculation examination cannot, by the standards of the day, be described as narrow: the inclusion of English and science represented a major addition to the diet of classics and a little mathematics served up in the contemporary public schools. The results of the first matriculation examination were published on 29 November 1838.* Twenty-two candidates passed and the exhibitions for classics and mathematics/natural philosophy were each divided between pairs of candidates.

The University of London matriculation examination was the progenitor of the British school examination system and of university entrance examinations in general. Its minimum age limit of 16 and

---

* The examination established a number of interesting firsts in examination organisation. The professor of the one candidate who failed wrote asserting that the chemistry questions were 'not to the syllabus': a Senate committee rejected the claim. Issues arose of comparability with the Oxbridge matriculation systems but these were deemed to be of inferior quality. A statistical record was started which noted the name, residence, age, college and place of birth (but not yet the sex) of the candidates. Lastly, the regulations and examination papers were put on public sale, price one shilling.

remainder of the 19th-century exhibitions and scholarships were awarded on the results of the basic matriculation examination.

• In 1863 the first blind candidate was examined. The papers were read to him and he dictated his answers to an amanuensis.

• The first overseas matriculation examination was conducted in Mauritius in 1865. Within twenty years the examinations of the university were being conducted at centres throughout the British Empire.

• In 1868, just thirty years after the first University of London matriculation examination, it was attracting over seven hundred entries a year. Despite, what by modern standards would be considered a very modest candidature, the desire to devise a fair system of examination had already prompted many of the problems that face today's Chief Examiners. The matriculation examination had already been organised on a subject group basis – a system that will be familiar to all who have taken School Certificate and Higher School Certificate.

It was the need for the University of London to regulate entry to its degree courses that laid, almost by accident, the foundations of our current systems of school examinations. The early examinations of the university – especially the matriculation examination – established basic ideas and approaches to public examinations which persist to this day. As the century proceeded, institutions of education throughout England, then the British Isles, and within forty years the British Empire, came to enter their students for the examinations of the university. Not all of the students went on to study for a degree, and the pre-degree examinations of the university came to be used for other than university purposes. The examinations became recognised measures of educational attainment. The origins of the current 16+ system of school examinations – the General Certificate of Secondary Education, (GCSE) – can be traced directly to the University of London matriculation examination which was introduced in 1838. The origins of current 18+ examinations – the General Certificate of Education advanced and advanced supplementary level examinations, GCE A and AS levels – can be traced directly to the same university's intermediate examinations introduced in 1858.

18+ origins: the intermediate examination

The expansion of knowledge and the development of new courses led the University of London from 1858 to expand the period of study required for the BA degree to three years. A two-part examination was introduced: the first part, designed to be taken one year after matriculation, became variously called the 'part 1', the 'preliminary' and lastly the 'intermediate' examination. The examination gave rise in time to the higher school certificate (HSC) and GCE advanced level examinations. The degrees in science introduced a year later also used the same examination structure.

The intermediate examination was a faculty examination and therefore far more specialised than matriculation. This, essentially university examination, became the model for later English 18+ school examinations and the direct cause of the narrowness of the modern sixth form curriculum.

Early school examinations

As the 19th century progressed the need arose for examinations which reflected the education provided in the better secondary schools. Neither the traditional classical education nor a scheme aimed at university entrance were appropriate for all students. The school, or local, examinations introduced by Oxford in 1857, by Cambridge one year later and by London in 1874 were an attempt to fulfil the need.

All three universities used similar systems of specially appointed examiners who were empowered to inspect the school, set examinations and award prizes. The systems were never popular with the teaching profession who considered the university examiners out of touch with the realities of the classroom. From the mid-1870s onwards pressure arose for the establishment of matriculation standard examinations for schools.

School Certificate and Higher School Certificate

Before 1900 the role of the University of London was still only that of an examining board so teaching for the intermediate examination took place in the same educational institutions that taught for the matriculation and/or degree examinations. Indeed, the distinction that we see today between secondary and higher education institutions was less clear in the 19th century; some institutions that we would now recognise as secondary schools may well have taught to degree level, similarly, many institutions that became today's universities taught to matriculation standard well into the 1930s. This overlap between institutions of secondary and higher education served to maintain the basic problem with the 18+ curriculum; the examination at the end of the two year period of sixth form study (although usually school based) was in aims, in design and in organisation a relatively narrow, university dominated one.

The 1902 Education Act made provision for the establishment of a national school certificate system, but it was not fully operational until 1917. In the meantime a number of school certificate boards were established, usually based upon individual or groups of universities. The examination was intended to be both a school leaving certificate and an entrance qualification for universities and the professions. The results of both the School Certificate and later the Higher School Certificate were reported in terms of marks but at each level ranges of marks served as *de facto* grades.

The minimum standard required for a school certificate pass was, what we would now consider to be the very modest mark of 30%. Marks of 45% and above were termed 'credits' and 70% and above 'distinctions'. Students could pass 'School Cert' if they obtained the required combinations of subject passes. They could pass 'matric' if they obtained the required numbers of credits. Only schools that were inspected by the new boards were able to enter their students for the School Certificate. Indeed, maintained schools were not allowed to enter their students for any other examinations – the SC and HSC were known as the 'First' and 'Second Approved Examinations' respectively. Students who did not attend such institutions were still able to qualify for university entrance by taking the continuing matriculation examinations of the University of London and others.

The years between the 1902 Education Act and the establishment of a national school certificate system were ones of experimentation with 16+, but not 18+, examinations. The new boards did not all immediately adopt the same style of examination that they had used for matriculation examination, i.e. with syllabuses and papers set by the board (what we would now call a mode 1 examination). Other forms of examination were also tried. The University of London initially required its school inspectors to set and mark special papers for each school, papers that reflected the teaching given – what we now call a mode 2 examination. The method could only function with a limited number of schools. As more schools took part in the School Certificate system the teachers came to be involved in the development of syllabuses and the setting of examination papers (mode 3). Given the transport systems of the day, it was very difficult for teachers from other than a limited number of schools to work together to develop syllabuses and write examination papers and this mode of examination also became unworkable as school-based examinations increased. By the time of the First World War, mode 1 examinations had become the norm.

The 1902 Act also established the Secondary Schools Examinations Council – the SSEC – whose function was the regulation of the School Certificate system. The Council approved school examination boards and vetted their procedures.

The developing school certificate boards also gradually established Higher School Certificate examinations, the HSC – again restricted to students in school that were under inspection by the boards. Passing the HSC could grant exemption from the universities' intermediate examinations, indeed in the early years of the London HSC examinations the candidates took the same papers as those sitting the intermediate examination. The HSC was therefore a specialist examination designed with the potential university entrant clearly in mind and students were usually required to opt for combinations of either arts or science subjects.

The Higher School Certificate examinations of some universities were not so closely tied to their intermediate examinations. As a result not all universities were prepared to grant automatic 'inter exemption' to students that had passed the HSC of another university. This situation continued until 1938 when mutual recognition of HSCs was agreed with one exception, biology. The University of London did not recognise other boards' HSC, and later A level, examinations in this subject for 1st MB exemption until 1960!

The start of the School Certificate and Higher School Certificate opened up two main routes from school to the final part of a university degree. The first route, the one most commonly used by the traditional university entrant – the pupil from the grammar or independent school – was via the SC and HSC, the second was via matriculation and intermediate examinations. Other routes were possible as figure 1 indicates. Students could, for example, proceed to the intermediate examination having either passed the SC examination and entered university, or passed matriculation using combinations of 'matric' and 'highers' subjects. It was when World War 1 ended and demobilised soldiers filled the available places in higher education institutions that the HSC route to a degree became established. By the mid-1920s it was dominant.

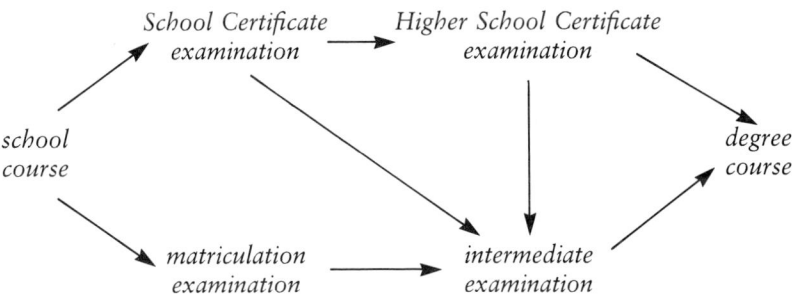

Figure 1 *Routes to university degree courses 1918–1951*

By 1922 there were eight boards conducting HSC examinations in England and Wales:

- Northern Universities Joint Matriculation Board
- Oxford and Cambridge Schools Examination Board
- University of London
- Central Welsh Board
- University of Cambridge Syndicate for Local Examinations
- University of Oxford Delegacy for Local Examinations
- University of Durham
- University of Bristol

Up to the mid-1930s, the period of the HSC was not noted as one of curriculum innovation. There were some developments in the numbers of subjects examined and methods of assessment, e.g. orals and practicals, but generally the need to pass in prescribed combinations of subjects seems to have inhibited curriculum innovation.

The structure of the Higher School Certificate was complicated. In the 1938 regulations of the University of London, candidates had to satisfy the examiners in one of five groups of subjects (although most subjects occurred in more than one group):

Group A: classics
Group B: modern languages (French, German, Spanish, Italian or Russian), English, history, geography, music, economics, art and religious studies
Group C: mathematics (pure and applied)
Group D: sciences and geography
Group E: modern languages (French, German, Spanish, Italian or Russian), mathematics, humanities

(The system of subject groups are discontinued by most boards after the mid-1930s.)

There were no grades as such; successes were reported in terms of marks. The certificates recorded only 'main passes' (40 marks or more) and 'main passes with distinction' (75 or more). There was also a 'subsidiary level pass' awarded in most subject groups to those who obtained 30 to 39% of the marks. In groups A, B, D, and E candidates had to pass a minimum of three main subjects, and in Group C two main and two subsidiary subjects at the same examination, to be awarded their certificate and obtain 'inter exemption'. Three main subject passes, or two main and two 'subsid' passes became the norm. Candidates tended to play safe by entering for four or five main subjects in the hope of obtaining the required combinations of passes.

The examination was university orientated; the syllabuses and permitted combinations of subjects were dictated by faculty requirements and the papers were set by university staff. The rigidity of the choices at 18+ probably reinforced the trend towards specialisation at School Certificate level and may have inhibited curriculum development throughout the secondary school.

Despite its university orientation, the Higher School Certificate examinations did achieve recognition as a general educational qualification. Those who passed the HSC were able to enter the army, and local government and the Civil Service at a higher grade than those with only School Certificate. Students who failed to gain sufficient main and/or subsidiary passes to qualify for the HSC were granted 'letters of success' for those subjects in which they did achieve passes. The system did permit a small measure of flexibility. Some universities allowed passes to be carried forward from one examination to another in exceptional cases, and some allowed a mixture of School Certificate and Higher School Certificate subject passes to provide matriculation exemption.

Once the Higher School Certificate was established it became the basis on which many local educational authority, national and endowed scholarships were awarded. The most well known of these, the State Scholarship scheme, was instituted in 1920. It was quite possible for students to hold scholarships from both their LEAs and other bodies. The link between particular LEAs and boards through the scholarship system meant that the maintained schools in that LEA did not have freedom to choose their examining board. From 1937, first the NUJMB and within a few years four other boards introduced special scholarship papers which were taken in addition to the HSC. These papers were intended to improve the discrimination of the examination at the top end of the HSC ability range – shades of the University of London matriculation honours papers. Each year, each board was given a quota of scholarships to award on the basis of candidates' best three, and later two, results.

In 1937 the Secondary School Examinations Council published a report into the Higher School Certificate, produced by a committee chaired by Cyril Norwood. This report noted the expansion that was taking place in entries for the HSC, looked forward to the expansion of the role of the sixth form and tried to define the ways in which main and subsidiary subjects might be used to fulfil the needs of different groups of students within the sixth form. Generally, however, the report seems to have endorsed the concept of specialisation for the potential university entrant without great reservation. It expressed the rather complacent view that 'as the university authorities are by no means discontented with the material which reaches them' there was little need for fundamental changes. The 1937 SSEC report acknowledged the need for a broader sixth form curriculum, but not of course at the expense of specialisation, and focused on the subsidiary subjects as the method of achieving its aims. Subsidiary studies could, it was suggested, fulfil roles as:

(a) *Ancillary subjects.* The study of a subsidiary subject could, it was suggested, support more intensive study in another subject. Examples cited included: mathematics as an ancillary subject to physics; and, Latin to modern languages.

(b) *Subjects to be valued in their own right.* It was reasoned that some subjects might be included in a combination of two main and two subsidiary choices, not to support specialist study in a cognate area but, as a contribution to the students general academic education.

(c) *Relief subjects.* The report noted the practice of many schools to offer their students 'contrasting' courses, often as non-examination subjects and this concept was endorsed by the SSEC.

The meaning of the term 'contrasting' in (c) above differs from that inherent in the contemporary phrase 'contrasting AS levels' (see page 94). The latter usage is nearer to (b) above. The 1937 meaning of the term has undertones of fun and enjoyment. Unfortunately, no examples were offered (or implemented).

The SSEC report anticipated the recommendations of the 1960 Crowther Report and suggested that only two-thirds to three-quarters of the sixth form curriculum should be devoted to study for the HSC examinations. It also proposed that subsidiary subjects should represent a standard half-way between School Certificate and Higher School Certificate examinations. Subsidiary subjects should be taught and examined alongside main (the report's term was 'principal') subjects. Thus both HSC types of papers should be taken after five terms of study. It was to take nearly 50 years for some of these proposals to be implemented. (There are some traditionalists who would see this as undue haste.) The only respect in which subsidiary subjects were to be considered as being of lesser value was that they, the SSEC report recommended, would not have been used in the award of State Scholarships.

The report also expressed concerns about variations in the examination boards in both the demands made upon students – attention was drawn to differences in the boards' science practical examinations – and the standards of the examinations, especially in the subsidiary subjects. The members of the committee were strongly opposed to the imposition of rigid rules for public examinations and recognised the consensus nature of standards. With these views in mind, the SSEC 1937 report went on to suggest that it was through the gradual improvement of the examination system, rather than through major changes, that developments would best be achieved.

In several ways the 1937 SSEC report had anticipated the corresponding developments of 50 years on. It proposed new roles for subsidiary subjects – to broaden both the curriculum of indvidual students and of the sixth form population as a whole. It advocated the evolutionary development of school examinations, and this were to prove to be a potent force for change during the period of the advanced level examination.

It is difficult now to assess the breadth of the curriculum which underpinned the HSC – it was perhaps the public perceptions of the examination that were narrow. In 1938 a committee of the Board of Education reviewed 'The organistion and curriculum of sixth forms in secondary education'. The report noted that most students went on to:

- University
- (Teachers') Training College
- Technology College
- Commercial College
- College of Domestic Science or Art or Music, and the Nursing Profession
- The Civil Service
- Commerce
- Industry

The report also recorded that in 'girls schools there is a considerable group who on leaving school are called upon to devote themselves to home duties' (p. 6).

Prior to World War II entries for the HSC were not high and for many schools the examination was seen as servicing the needs of the most able only. Failure to take (or to pass) HSC did not exclude students from entering university; that could still be achieved by School Certificate passes to 'matric' standard or via special university entrance examinations for mature students. 16+ examinations remained the significant school examination – a situation which is only being seriously challenged today. Thus 18+ examinations could be permitted to be specialist because 16+ examinations ensured (to some extent) the general element of education.

Educational standards in the SC and HSC systems do not appear to have been quite as high as those of today. Without our current system of financial support grants for higher education, selection for higher education had to be made on financial criteria as well as academic ones. It was not unusual to see students starting university courses, albeit at 'pre-inter' standard, with qualifications that today would just be deemed adequate for admission to the academic sixth form of some of the more selective schools. In the 1930s it was not uncommon to see some of the nation's prestigious medical schools advertising their successes at matriculation.

Just four years later in 1943, a second SSEC committee reconsidered the school examination system as a whole. (This second report was also chaired by Cyril Norwood and has passed into history as 'the Norwood Report'.) It developed further the idea of a broader sixth form curriculum – a development that may well have been related to the start of World War II. Could it be that the skills required of its most able youngsters by a nation at war were not all to be found in an over-specialised sixth form education?

The General Certificate of Education ordinary and advanced levels

The 1943 Norwood Report also proposed the replacement of the School and Higher School Certificate examinations by single subject examinations. The new examinations, the General Certificate of Education ordinary and advanced levels were introduced in 1951. The Higher School Certificate main subject syllabuses became, without modification, the first A level ones. The HSC subsidiary and SC syllabuses were absorbed into the O level system. Three A levels became the norm for university entrance so the GCE A level curriculum was thus even narrower than the HSC one. The GCE system was firmly based on the existing pattern of grammar school education. Initially, there was no special provision for further education students – they were expected to take the same subjects, and numbers of subjects, as the grammar school students.

At both levels the concept of subject groups was done away with and candidates – in particular their schools and colleges – were able to make a free choice of syllabuses, although expectations about subject combinations remain to this day. Students (and schools) were free to select subjects from more than one board, but few did so at first.

The most revolutionary aspects of the GCE system were the award of certificates to candidates who passed even a single subject and the abolition of the minimum ages of entry. The GCE was planned as a pass/fail examination and in the early years the results were communicated in the form of marks. At A level, as with the previous HSC examinations, 40% constituted a pass, and 75% a distinction. The designers of the examination believed that the more able students would proceed directly to A levels and not take O levels first – a system called 'by-passing'. To accommodate the student who took the A level examinations but did not quite reach the required pass standard, an O level pass could be awarded.

The first GCE examinations also inherited the style and attitudes inherent in the SC and HSC system. The O and A level syllabuses were short by modern standards and content-orientated. The early A level examinations were university dominated in their syllabus design, procedures and forms of examination. The examination papers typically contained two, and at the most three, papers. The questions were usually essays, with an emphasis on recall.

The change to the GCE partly coincided with, and partly accelerated, the expansion of examinations at both levels. Nevertheless, the old attitudes and methods of working rapidly proved inadequate. They had worked well in a relatively closed, academic (and some might even say cosy) system in which: almost all A level teachers were themselves the product of the university system; most of the pupils came from grammar and independent schools; and university places were limited. They became less appropriate as: the numbers of students; the variety of institutions from which they came; and the needs of society in general, all changed. Not that the A level received an entirely favourable response when it was introduced, it was criticised for two main failings:

(a) for the narrowness of the sixth form curriculum that led up to the A level examination – we shall consider the validity of this criticism and attempts to resolve it in Chapter 3;

(b) for technical inefficiency – we shall consider how these criticisms were resolved in Chapter 4.

did ease in the latter part of the 1970s and further during the 1980s, when it was realised that it had been remarkably successful and, it was realised that Britain generally had one of the lowest proportions of students staying on to 18+. By that time, however, attitudes about what universities expected were ingrained.

Early in the history of the A level examination attempts to improve the sixth form took the form of recommendations/agreements to broaden the curriculum with liberal and general studies courses. Although these recommendations came to be accepted as models of good practice, they were unenforceable, lacking the direct link with examinations.

Other pressures for change often expressed themselves in dissatisfaction with individual features of the A level system and thereby tended to blur the basic issues. Examples were: pressures to introduce new subjects; and, general pressures to update syllabuses and assessment techniques. There were opposing pressures for increased teacher involvement in the examination process which contrasted with moves towards the increased centralisation of the examination process. There were also constant discussions about the use of examined and non-examined time. Many significant changes did take place (see Chapter 4) within the area of syllabus and examination development but most left the structure unchanged.

The main reports and proposals which sought to influence A levels were, in chronological order:

- Crowther report (published 1959, see CACE, 1959)
- The Agreement to Broaden the Curriculum (ABC) (introduced 1961, see MacFarlane, 1988)
- The General Studies Movement (1963 onwards, see MacFarlane, 1988)
- The Robbins Report (1963)
- Major/minor/general subjects (proposed 1966, see Schools Council, 1966)
- The International Baccalaureate Examination (introduced 1968, see Blackburn, 1988; and IBO, 1985)
- Elective subjects (proposed 1967, see Schools Council, 1967b)
- Qualifying and Further subjects (proposed 1969, see Schools Council 1969)
- Alternative Ordinary level (introduced 1976, see Schools Council, 1973b)

- Normal and Further subjects (proposed 1973, see Schools Council 1973b)
- Intermediate level (proposed 1980, see DES, 1980b)
- Advanced Supplementary level (introduced 1989, see DES, 1984)
- 'Leaner and tougher A levels': the Higginson proposals (DES, 1988c)

- The SEAC proposals for the reform of the advanced (A and AS)
  level system (1989/90, see SEAC, 1990b)

The Higher School Certificate

The A level examination was a development from a previous system,
the Higher School Certificate (HSC), which can be described as a
slightly wider and broader examination than its successor. Students
of the former often took four or five subjects hoping to gain the
necessary combinations of either three main subject passes or two
main plus two subsidiary passes. Teachers had no role in the assessment process except to submit assessments of practical or oral work
which might have been used in borderline cases.

Although the 1937 SSEC report expressed great concerns about
the narrowness of the HSC examination and had acknowledged the
possible development of the 'new sixth form', early A levels were by
contrast even more specialist, concentrating on three main subjects
from the same cognate area. The early GCE system made very little
provision for students from colleges of further education or those
wanting to take combinations of 16+ or 18+ courses. The subsidiary
HSC syllabuses, where they existed, were absorbed into the O level
examination.

The introduction of the A level prompted immediate concerns
about its greater narrowness and only slightly increased flexibility,
but these were initially overshadowed – as already indicated in Chapter 2 – by greater worries about the general technical efficiency of
the examination.

The Crowther Report

In 1959 the Central Advisory Council for England was established:

> to consider in relation to the changing social and industrial needs of our
> society, and the needs of its individual citizens, education of boys and
> girls between 15 and 18, and in particular to consider the balance at
> various levels of general and specialised studies between these ages and
> to examine the interrelationship of the various stages of education. (Page
> xxvii in the preface to Vol. I)

The main recommendations of the report (Central Advisory Council for England, 1959) of interest here concerned the curriculum of
the traditional sixth form. The report gave very little attention to the
practicalities of broadening the curriculum of the A level examination
– indeed it had very little at all to say about the examination. It
also ignored the 'new sixth' which was already appearing. A broad

education was proposed but not at the expense of A level specialisation. The Committee advocated teacher/pupil 'discipleship' through individual supervision. It was recommended that students should not sit more than three A level subjects and that a substantial part of their time should be spent on non-examination courses and activities. One of the major effects of the publication of the report was thus support for the concept of sixth form general studies which, paradoxically, tended to become an examination subject.

The report made some contradictory suggestions about the roles of teachers. While emphasising their potential contribution to the education of pupils through such developments as liberal and general studies courses, it nevertheless did not see them having a role in the A level assessment process.

Some questions must be asked about the practicability of the ideas that were proposed. The value of non-examined general studies and interest courses had been demonstrated within some grammar and independent schools, which in a time of teacher shortage had no problems of recruitment. The practicability of extending such ideas to all schools and colleges was doubtful. Like the agreement on minority time the recommendations were unenforceable except through the inspectorate. Lastly, competition for places in higher education was extremely high and this might also have inhibited innovation. Pressure for high A level grades is likely to have diminished the value of non-examined time in the eyes of some students and teachers.

The Crowther Report must be seen as the last expression of the value of specialisation. It may also have served to divert attention from the main path towards a broader sixth form curriculum by endorsing the idea of non-examined courses.

The agreement to broaden the curriculum (ABC)

In the mid to late 1950s a group of secondary school headmasters reached an informal agreement to reserve one third of the sixth form curriculum for studies outside the usual diet of A level subjects and physical education. They formalised this policy, introduced in 1961, under the title of 'the agreement on minority time'. A leader of this movement was Mr A.D.C. Peterson, then headmaster of Dover Grammar School. The other schools involved were drawn from the major public and established grammar schools of the day.

The agreement in minority time was nothing more than the name implied. Its voluntary nature obviously excluded the possibility of the agreement becoming anything other than an accepted model of good practice. Those involved could only influence other schools and each other through the power of argument, and powerful arguments were needed. The schools already involved tended to be those with the greatest resources – of time, of space and, most importantly, of people – to implement the agreement. For schools of lower status this was a time of teacher shortage and it was often difficult, given the pressure of examination courses, to make the time available to plan and implement worthwhile general studies courses. 1959 saw two important developments: the publication of the Crowther Report (see above) and C.P. Snow's famous Reith Lecture on the two cultures (Allanson *et al.*, 1967). Snow drew attention to the divide between the sciences and the arts and proposed that 'science students be more literate' and that art specialists be more 'numerate'. This division of the curriculum into literate and numerate divisions was to colour thinking for several decades.

MacFarlane (1988) saw two events as crucial in the creation of a coherent general studies movement. Firstly, in 1961, 360 Head-masters of public and maintained schools signed an Agreement to Broaden the Curriculum (ABC) and pledged themselves to meet within two years Crowther's recommendation, that one third of the sixth form timetable should be devoted to non-specialist studies; this being in addition to time spent on physical education and private study. Secondly, in 1962 the SSEC published a report entitled *Sixth Form Studies and University Entrance Requirements* (SSEC, 1962), which make a distinction between course and general entrance requirements. The former, it was agreed, should remain at least two A level passes. With respect to the second, the SSEC report proposed the possible examining of 'use of English' and general studies as a means of ensuring adequate communication skills and breadth of study in potential university entrants. In a letter to the Vice Chancel-lors and Principals of the Universities of the United Kingdom, the Headmasters' Conference and Joint Four associations expressed some worries about the validity of the former. The five organisations endorsed the concept of examined general studies and also proposed the idea that individual school's sixth form general studies pro-grammes might be 'accredited' for university entrance purposes. The 'use of English' papers were introduced by some university exami-nation boards but did not prove to be particularly popular, unless they were supported by clear statements in university entrance requirements. General studies courses for examination at A or AO level were, however, developed by most boards.

The SSEC report also discussed the possible introduction of 'use of a foreign language' papers as part of general requirements. The five teachers' associations expressed clear preferences for any such introduction of compulsory foreign languages into the sixth form to be restricted to unseen translations and comprehension tests, along the lines of then existing university language competence tests. All five associations, nevertheless, also expressed the view that attempts should be made to maintain foreign language competency in the sixth form minority subject programme through wide reading.

In 1963 the General Studies Association was formed following three head teachers' conferences organised by the Oxford Institute of Education. Once again, Mr Peterson played an important part in these developments. The establishment of the association clearly put general studies on the sixth form timetable for almost all students, although as MacFarlane (1988) points out, very few schools and colleges achieved the target of one third timetable provision.

There have always been, and probably will remain, two fundamental problems with sixth form general studies. The first is that no clear consensus exists as to what general studies is supposed to be about. It is generally assumed that it is an important counterweight to the specialism of A level courses, as it requires students to address wider issues and to work along side colleagues from other specialist areas. Other teachers have viewed general studies as an opportunity to teach general inter-disciplinary skills which will be of value in higher education and employment. The second problem with general studies has been to providing the intellectual stimulation and teaching resources in all sixth forms. Where the value of general studies is appreciated and the determination to broaden sixth form curriculum in this way exists, the resources have usually been found. However, not all sixth forms have been blessed with staff with the enthusiasm to introduce the subject and the ability to design appropriate courses. As a result, where the concept of general studies has been endorsed but development has not been possible, work has tended to focus upon the syllabuses prepared by the examination boards.

From the early 1960s to the present day there have been tensions between teachers who have wished to design their own general studies courses (which until recently have usually been non-examination courses) and those who have wanted to broaden the sixth form curriculum via the GCE boards' examination courses in the subject. This tension is often related to the general width of the sixth form curriculum and shows distinct regional variations in its resolution. In the north of England, focusing on the examinations of the Joint Matriculation Board (JMB), the typical pattern of A level subjects has tended to be three specialist subjects – often in very traditional combinations – with a fourth A level in general studies. Further south, the same desire to broaden the curriculum of the sixth form has lead to more students taking cross-curricular combinations of subjects and general studies, where it is examined, often being taken at AO level.

General studies remains an important force in sixth form education to the present day. Indeed, the subject was one of the five that were endorsed and sponsored by the Government during recent AS level developments. Nevertheless, the existence of the general studies movement has in some ways distracted attention from the need for fundamental structural reform of the A level system.

The Robbins Report (Robbins, 1963)

The Robbins Committee was commissioned by the then Prime Minister Harold Macmillan to review the pattern of full time higher education in Britain. The committee reported in 1963 just prior to a general election and both major parties pledged themselves to implement its recommendations. The report had very little to say about the examination system but, in successfully recommending a mammoth expansion of higher education, closed the door on radical changes to the structure of A level for many years. There were insufficient resources for both the expansion of higher education *and* any reforms of school examinations, that might lead to the extension of higher education courses.

The creation of new universities and polytechnics, rather than reducing the competitiveness of the higher education entry process, also serve to increase students' awareness of such opportunities. New universities and polytechnics, new courses, new thinking about sixth form courses all resulted from the expansion and so indirectly the Robbins report served to increase pressures for change and development within the A level system.

The Robbins Report also recommended research into the development of a scholastic aptitude test – an assessment device commonly used in the USA for college entrance. The Schools Council in association with the committee of University Vice Chancellors and Principals (CVCP) expressed the hope in 1964 that such a test would supplement other forms of evidence used in the United Kingdom university entrance process. The vice chancellors believed that an 18+ aptitude test would become an increasing aid to assessing the comparability of the different GCE boards' A level examinations – an issue which was receiving increasing public attention at the time. Both hopes proved to be misplaced – the issues turned out to be unexpectedly complex. Nevertheless the research stimulated, at least in part by the Robbins Report, did lead gradually to the idea that a variety of assessment techniques should be used in A level examinations. The concept of variety led in turn to improvements in the quality of English school examinations and became their most distinctive characteristic.

discussed. They would also have been practicable for, with the omission of the general studies component, they were to reappear as the GCE Advanced Supplementary (AS) level proposals which became operational in 1989. One significant difference between the major/minor/general proposals and the eventually implemented AS level examination, was the amount of time that the former recommended should be devoted to non-examination studies. By 1989 the value attached to non-examination work in the sixth form had been diminished.

The development of the International Baccalaureate

The International Baccalaureate Organisation (IBO) was started in 1968 with Alex Peterson as a founding member and as first director. From the start the IBO reflected Peterson's major concern with a rounded sixth form education but with an international dimension.

The IBO is now associated in everybody's minds with the International Baccalaureate examination and diploma which has become – throughout the independent school sector, some schools and colleges in the UK and elsewhere – an internationally recognised qualification and rival to the GCE advanced level system. The IB provides a recognised pre-university curriculum and the IB diploma gives access to higher education almost worldwide. The curriculum and examinations were developed in the belief that 'international education is not a luxury but a necessity in an increasingly independent and multi-cultural world' (International Baccalaureate Office, 1985). The IB examination provides international schools in particular with a common curriculum at upper secondary and matriculation level by a standardised system of education it offers opportunities for parents who have become increasingly internationally mobile to see their children educated overseas whilst still retaining their ability to return to higher education in their own countries.

The curriculum and examination is based on six subject groups.

Group 1

Language A (first language). Students will choose their best language – either their mother tongue or the language of the school and through this medium study a course in world literature which accounts for 30% of the language A mark. The purpose of the first language is to ensure that those who wish to, may return to higher education in their own country.

Group 2

Language B (second language or a second language A). For most students language B will be a language which is foreign to them. The study of the second language is also obligatory.

Group 3

Study of man in society. A choice of history, geography, economics, philosophy, psychology, social anthropology, organisation and management studies.

Group 4

Experimental sciences. A choice of biology, chemistry, applied chemistry, physics, physical science, experimental psychology, environmental systems.

Group 5

Mathematics. A choice of mathematics, mathematics with computing, mathematical studies, mathematics with further mathematics.

Group 6

One of the following options:

(a) arts/design, music, Latin, classical Greek, or computing studies
(b) a school based syllabus approved by the IBO.

Alternatively, a candidate can offer, instead of a group 6 subject, a third modern language, a second subject from the study of man in society, a second subject from the experimental sciences.

Of the six subjects in the IB system, students are expected to take three or four of them at the higher level and the remainder at subsidiary level. Higher level courses require 240 teaching hours each and subsidiary level subjects 150 teaching hours each.* In addition to their main and subsidiary course studies, all IB candidates are expected to undertake: an extended essay which may result in bonus points; papers in the theory of knowledge, which involves study of about 100 hours spread over two years and which is internally assessed; and, spend half a day per week on creative/affective studies in the social sciences (CASS). The last element involves about half a day a week. It is compulsory but not assessed.

IB grades and awards

At both higher and subsidiary level each examined subject is graded on a scale of one (minimum) to seven (maximum). Nominally the

---

* It is interesting to note that the time that would have been required to teach two subsidiary level subjects (2 × 150 hours) is considerably greater than the time required to teach one main subject.

award of the diploma requires a minimum total of 24 points but in practice the points awarded for the higher level courses have the determining effect. For example, it is not possible for a person to compensate for poor performances in higher level subjects, even if the highest points were obtained for their subsidiary subjects. In 1990 the IB is taken by some 500 schools – mostly international schools – in 54 countries. In the United Kingdom it is accepted as a general entrance requirement for university but in some cases high points in the higher level studies are required for admission to particular courses.

The IB examination illustrates some of the issues inherent in broadening the sixth form curriculum. The IB curriculum is significantly broader than the usual three A levels, but has it been bought at the cost of standards? Some university entrance tutors have noted that IB students are not always as well prepared as their A level peers within their specialist subjects. As the course progresses, however, their greater motivation and communication skills tend to permit them to excel. This observation may be more a result of the educational advantages and social background of the IB students rather than their inherent intellectual abilities. It is not clear whether this observation relates to particular parts of the curriculum or generally. What is also not so clear in the IB system is how well it serves the needs of those who are not destined for higher education courses. Unlike the A and AS level system, no awards are made for successes in just a few of the IB subjects.

Elective studies (1969)

The idea of school-designed and examination board-accredited (elective) general studies rearose directly from the discussions between the Schools Council and the Universities Standing Council on University Entrance (SCUE) about the major/minor/general proposals. In both sets of proposals, students would have been expected to study a specialist course equivalent to two A levels. The difference was, however, that the minor courses, which would have been the plank of the major/minor general proposals, were to be replaced by a battery of six internally assessed and externally moderated elective courses. Elective studies would in effect have been based on the mode 3 principle and each course would have been of one year's duration.

If elective subjects were to have played a full part in the university entrance process, two conditions would have had to have been met. Firstly, the content of the courses might, at least partly, have had to be prescribed. At the time the idea of giving teachers a major role in course design and assessment was popular with educationalists but was far less so with other groups. The idea of teachers exercising control over key aspects of the university admissions procedure was treated with suspicion by many, even if it were to be supported by a scholastic aptitude test of the sort suggested by Robbins. Secondly, a sophisticated moderation process would have been required. Either of these might have imposed such constraints upon the system to have impaired the spirit of elective subjects. Neither of these issues were resolved and the idea of elective studies was quickly dropped. The appearance of electives so soon after the major/minor/general proposals may well have distracted attention from the former.

The introduction of elective subjects might not have served to broaden the sixth form anyway. The technical problems inherent in the standardisation of courses could have meant that an even greater emphasis was placed upon the two A levels. It would have been difficult to maintain the quality of elective courses and they would have varied widely from one school to another. Perhaps for these reasons the later attempts to broaden the sixth form curriculum were all conducted in terms of directly examined subjects.

The attitude of the universities to a broader A level curriculum remained ambiguous. Dr E.W.H. Briault, Deputy Chief Education Officer of the Inner London Education Authority suggested in an interview for *The Times Educational Supplement* that the universities continued to speak with two voices: 'They all want to liberalise the sixth form curriculum but when it comes to individuals, each don demands high marks in his own particular subject (*TES*, 1967).

Qualifying and further levels (1969)

The search for a method of broadening the curriculum continued, after the rejections of the proposals for major/minor/general subjects and electives, with the establishment by the Schools Council and SCUE of a further working party in 1968. The working party reported in 1969 and suggested:

● that students should keep open a wide range of options until 17+;

● that all students study a broad curriculum at 16+. The most able students would continue to take eight O level subjects;

● that in the lower sixth the more able students should study about five broadly spread subjects and take a Qualifying Examination at 17+ (so called because it would become the general entrance requirement for higher education);

● that in the upper sixth students would devote their time to specialist studies in, typically, three F (further) level subjects.

There was some divisions among the members of the Committee

about the value to be attached to O level generally. Some felt that it would be appropriate for the examinations to wither away altogether while others felt that it should be replaced in significance by an examination at 17+.

The Working Party claimed that the strength of its proposals was that the system possessed flexibility. The traditional sixth formers would receive a broader based education to 17+ while still being able to specialise in three subjects at 18+. The needs of the new sixth form would have been well served by 17+ Q levels courses or mixtures of Q and some F level subjects. The Q and F proposals were radically different from previous proposals for broadening the sixth form curriculum and would have involved a restructuring of school/college organisation and teaching methods at 17+, 18+ and possibly even the 16+. There would have been major examinations at all three stages, with all that that implied.

The Q and F proposals were unpopular from the first. They were perceived as having four major, and interrelated problems. Firstly, if school examination did indeed take place at 16+, 17+ and 18+, the pressures on students and the disruption to school would have been considerable. Secondly, both the Q and F courses would have been short, in effect two and a bit terms. Thirdly, there were some doubts about the role of examinations at 16+. If the Q level became the basis of entry to higher education then what would have been the role of O level? If the importance of O level had diminished then the increasing emphasis attached to the Q level examination might have narrowed, rather than broadened, the sixth form curriculum. The role of general and liberal studies courses was also unclear and pressure from examination courses could well have reduced the time allocation. Lastly, there were concerns about the standards of the F level examination. With time being spent on extra subjects at Q level and given the short duration of F level courses, the standard of the latter would inevitably have been less than A level. Even in 1969 any tampering with A level standards was almost sacrilegious. The issue of standards prompted an immediate reaction by the universities that their courses would have to be lengthened to four years if Q and F levels were introduced. The proposals were thus effectively killed off by the higher education lobby.

The Working Party also proposed a single national body with overall responsibility for the Q and F examinations. This was not to have been an examining body but an agency for research, development and the administration of the new examination. The national body was to have oversight of the technical aspects of the examination and 'the kinds of lists of subjects' that the examination boards might offer. The concept was not, as might have been expected, popular with the GCE boards. Nevertheless, the numbers of subjects on offer, the numbers of syllabuses in key subjects and the standards of some new subjects were all used as justifications for increasing central control as the 1970s and 1980s passed.

Normal and further levels (1976)

By far the most fully researched of the ideas for the structural reform of 18+ examinations were the N and F level proposals. First suggested in 1973, the ideas were fully developed by 1976 (Schools Council, 1976). These proposals differed from the Q and F ones mainly in the fact that the former would not have involved an examination at 17+. Both N and F levels were to be two year courses. Typical students would have studied five subjects in the sixth form, perhaps two to the N level and the remainder to the higher F level.

Detailed studies were undertaken to assess the effects upon schools and individual students (Schools Council, 1978b) all with quite promising results. The N and F proposals would not, it appears, have demanded extra resources but would have lowered 18+ standards slightly. F levels would again have been of a slightly lower standard than A level – any reduction remained unacceptable to many people because of the possible implications for university courses. As a result the N and F proposals were rejected, for the now traditional reasons.

By this time those responsible for the sixth form A level curriculum felt themselves to be in an untenable position. As one said 'we are damned if we don't reform and damned if we try to!'

Examinations at 17+: the alternative ordinary level

The initial proposals for the O level examination had made a provision for shorter (one year) 'alternative' ordinary level courses for mature students. The O and A level systems were not proving sufficiently flexible to serve the needs of the 'new' sixth formers, increasing numbers of whom were joining each year. Early in the 1970s the Schools Council and the Examination Boards agreed to develop new courses for examination at 17+. The results were the alternative ordinary (AO) level organised by the GCE boards, and the Certificate of Extended Education (CEE) organised by the CSE boards on a pilot basis. The latter was planned as an examination for students who stayed on in school after taking the certificate of secondary education (CSE). The CEE and the rejuvenated AO level developed steadily from 1976. The AO level was not a true level but has frequently been spoken of as though it were. After 1976 most GCE boards reported AO level results separately. Unlike the CEE, AO level carried an official endorsement from the beginning. A consortium of GCE boards also came to offer the examination with each being responsible for one or two syllabuses.

The alternative ordinary level examination involved new syllabuses which were often shorter than the main O level ones but required greater maturity in the answers to examination questions. AO level syllabuses offered a fresh start for some former O level students, an opportunity for former CSE students to bridge the gap to A level work and all students an opportunity to broaden their sixth form courses. AO levels offered high-flyers with specialist interests – electronics, computing etc. – the opportunity to study 'interest' and 'supportive' subjects alongside more traditional O or A levels. In the early eighties, study for A and AO levels could also be combined with vocationally orientated courses such as those of Business and Technician Education Council (BTEC), City and Guilds of London Institute (CGLI), the Royal Society of Arts (RSA), and the Certificate for Pre-Vocational of Education (CPVE).

AO level courses proved to be popular during the late 1970s and 1980s, especially in mathematics and general studies. The ideas underpinning the AO level examination were a restatement of earlier principles. The very first university entrance examination to be conducted upon modern lines – the University of London matriculation examination – had offered an additional mathematics paper. The practice had continued providing an acknowledged step, often for high-flyers, between 16+ and 18+ examinations in the subject.

The origins of some of the AO level syllabuses can be traced back to the HSC supplementary syllabuses. Among these was anatomy, physiology and hygiene (APH), which was originally introduced as a pre-nursing course and evolved into the popular subject human biology. Many new syllabuses were introduced in the mid-1970s and after. The opportunity was taken to experiment with new subjects, new forms of syllabus organisation and new assessment techniques (e.g. teacher assessed work).

With the exception of additional mathematics syllabuses, the standards of the AO levels were those of O level and this was generally confirmed by the GCE boards' subject pairs analyses.* Over time, however, isolated instances came to light of underage students – 15 or even 14 year olds – whose teachers were attracted by the reduced syllabus content to enter them for the AO level examination. Some

---

* Subject of pairs analyses is a technique which the GCE boards use to explore inter-subject comparability. In short, the results of all candidates that have taken particular pairs of subjects are compared. Many apparent differences in standard inevitably result when individual pairings are considered. It is when a number of pairings consistently show that a particular subject is out of line with all of the others with which it could be successfully paired that corrective action tends to be taken. For further details see Forrest and Vickerman (1982).

of these students, although in all other respects good O level candidates, did very poorly at AO level examinations, lacking the maturity that the examination necessitated.

AO levels came to an end officially after 1988. Some were merged into GCSE (mature), others revised and expanded to become the bases of AS levels. The Cambridge Board, however, has retained the AO level examinations for mathematics on an unofficial basis until 1991. The certificate issued will not carry the signature of the Secretary of State for Education and Science reflecting this new status.

The CEE did not become established as a link between 16+ and 18+ courses in the same way as the GCE AO level did. Nevertheless, the opportunity was taken to experiment with new subjects and methods of assessment. Like AO levels, the CEE enjoyed a limited life after its official death. A consortium made up of the Cambridge, SUJB, O&C, and London GCE boards plus two CSE boards (the East Anglian Examinations Board and the London Regional Examination Board) developed a modular CEE system. Examinations were organised in 1989 and 1990 but insufficient candidates were forthcoming to allow the experiment to continue.

The intermediate level proposals

The CEE and the GCE AO level examinations were reviewed by the Keohane Committee in 1979 and their report was subsequently published (DES, 1980a). The Committee recommended the official recognition of 17+ examinations and, in effect, proposed a 17+ (intermediate) level; the idea was not taken up directly by the government.

The Keohane recommendations were considered in a consultative document *Examinations 16–18* (DES, 1980b) published by the Secretaries of State for Education and Science, and Wales. They reaffirmed their beliefs in contemporary A levels: as standards of academic excellence; as the foundation of degree courses; and, as the best means of selection for higher education. The Secretaries of State proposed that while A levels should continue for the foreseeable future, they expressed concerns about the degree of specialisation that the pursuit of good A levels and entrance to higher education tended to engender. Their proposed solution was the establishment of a new intermediate level examination to be taken alongside A levels. This new examination would require half the teaching and study time of A levels over two years. It was to be taught alongside A level rather than serve as a stepping stone between 16+ and 18+ courses as the term 'intermediate' seemed to imply.

Once again the ideas behind the new examination were a broadening of the students' studies by allowing them to replace one or more of their A level subjects by a larger number of the new I level courses. The concepts were far from new and were derived from the earlier minor subjects, which had been rejected. The I level proposals, however, received a guarded but positive response from employers, universities and the examination boards.

The GCE advanced supplementary level examination

By the early 1980s several factors that had inhibited structural change no longer applied. Firstly, the 'little Englander' and other attitudes still existed but they were outweighed by both the awareness that Britain was now part of Europe, and concepts about Britain as a trading nation. Therefore, it became acceptable to look critically at other people's ways of doing things. While acknowledging that the relationships between 18+ examinations and university entrance were different in most EEC countries, it was the higher proportion of students that stayed on to 18 and went into higher education (the participation rate) that caused most concern. Britain's participation rate was one of the lowest. Secondly, a decline in the numbers of young people, and the desire for a higher participation rate in higher education, was changing attitudes about school examinations and entry to higher education. These and other accountability arguments served to change attitudes. The value of breadth of study was re-emphasised, although the case presented for it was no better. Examinations came to be seen not as hurdles but as summative and formative assessments, with an emphasis on the positive qualities that a student had acquired from a course of study.

In May 1984, a further consultative document entitled *AS Levels* (DES, 1984) was published, again by the Secretaries of State for Education and Science, and Wales. This document expanded on the concept of the intermediate examination, now renamed the Advanced Supplementary level. Once again the approach to broadening the sixth form curriculum was to offer students half credit courses. Students were to be invited to replace one of their three A levels by two or more AS level subjects.

The new examinations were to require half the teaching and study time of A levels but were designed to achieve the same degree of academic rigour, although this term was not defined. Broadening of the sixth form curriculum was to be achieved by the simple addition of more subjects. There were two important strategies in the AS level model. Firstly, students were to have the opportunity of studying AS levels which both complemented and contrasted with their area of specialist study. This idea had also been carried forward from previous attempts at structural reform. Secondly, it was obvious that the Government viewed some subjects as having a more important role in broadening the sixth form curriculum than others. The Government sponsored the development of syllabuses in mathematics, English, modern languages, design and technology, and general studies.

The AS level syllabuses were intended to be very flexible. Although it was hoped that most of the traditional sixth form students whose sights were on higher education would take two specialist A levels with at least one contrasting AS level subject, other students would be able to make up sixth form courses using any combination of A and AS level studies.

The AS level proposals incorporated a number of controversial features and these related to the resources required to implement the ideas. Firstly, the Government expressed the hope that when developed, AS level syllabuses would be 'co-teachable' with A level syllabuses. In short, it was hoped that AS level students would be able to attend A level classes for those periods or aspects of the work that were common to both examinations. Secondly, it was hoped that the AS level syllabuses could be examined by drawing upon some of the components of the A level examinations. This second concept was later developed into an idea that A and AS level students should perform equally on common examination papers, sections and questions – a concept which is discounted in Chapter 5 as theoretically and practically unworkable. Both of the features pointed quite clearly to the AS level examination requiring two years of study in the sixth form rather than one.

While there were many reservations among the teaching profession to the concept of co-teaching, and from the examination boards to the concepts of common components and sections, neither of these criticisms were allowed to qualify the general welcome given to the AS level proposals. Nevertheless, both of these areas of concern were later to have implications for the implementation of the examination (see Chapter 5). The go-ahead for the AS level examination was given in *Better Schools* (DES, 1986a) and syllabus development began immediately. The first AS level examinations took place in 1989.

The quickening pace of 18+ reform: the Higginson Report

The introduction of AS levels is not the end of our story, far from it. Even before the AS level syllabuses were arriving in the schools, the Government announced the establishment of the Higginson Committee which was to undertake a review of A level examinations. The

FOUR

The evolution of advanced level examinations

Since their introduction in 1951 A level examinations have evolved. One has only to skim through the earliest and current syllabuses to see that the latter are more comprehensive, more clearly structured and make use of more (and more varied) assessment techniques. The latest syllabuses also make quite different demands on students and their teachers. In the 1950s, knowledge of content and vocabulary, and the ability to structure them in a reasonable essay, were frequently all that was required; in 1990 these are assumed and used in the development of higher order intellectual skills. Perhaps the most obvious, but rather superficial, comparison of the first and most recent A level syllabuses is the sheer space that they occupy. The syllabuses of 1951 were recorded in a few lines, seldom amounting to more than a page. The A level syllabuses of 1990, on the other hand, can occupy up to 30 or so pages. Further, the 1990 AS level syllabuses, while they are shorter than the corresponding A level ones, are often more complex than A level syllabuses of the mid-1970s.

The story of the development of the advanced level system largely reflects the characteristics of the bodies that have overseen it:

- 1951 to 1964, the Secondary Schools Examination Council (SSEC)

- 1964 to 1983, the Schools Council

- 1983 to 1988, the Secondary Examinations Council (SEC)

- 1988 onwards, the School Examinations and Assessment Council (SEAC)

There are two developments associated with the last two bodies listed above which between them will radically change the nature of advanced level examining in the coming decade(s). The first has been the introduction of AS levels and the second the passing of the 1988

Education Reform Act. The effects of the first upon 18+ examinations are obvious and immediate. The effects of the second, although it had little directly to say about the advanced level system, changed almost everything else.

18+ developments under the SSEC (1951 to 1964)

The SSEC dated from the 1902 Education Act and this latter part of its life – like the rest – was unexciting. The SSEC saw its role as policing the GCE system. It appears, in contrast to the other three bodies which have overseen the Advanced level system, to have been rather more bureaucratic and conservative.

The first A level syllabuses for examination were simply the Higher School Certificate ones renamed. Syllabuses were brief, and mainly content orientated. The examination structures were by today's ideas, simple, and typically consisted of two papers. In most subjects essay questions predominated. Initially, there was only one pass level which was defined in terms of 40% of the final marks. Different levels of performance were indicated using marks. If a student obtained 75% or more of the marks his or her certificate was endorsed 'pass with distinction'.

There were many initial criticisms of the A level examination. The new examination was narrower. It failed to make provision for students from colleges of further education or the slowly appearing 'new' sixth form. All the subsidiary higher school certificate subjects had been amalgamated, with the schools certificate syllabuses into the ordinary level examination. Secondly, there were doubts about its technical efficiency. Essay questions in particular were criticised. The earlier work of Hartog and Rhodes (1936) was receiving renewed public attention as a result of the popular psychology book written by Professor Hans Eysenck (1953). Nevertheless, the candidature for the A level examination rose steadily during these early years and members of the traditional sixth form still predominated.

During the 1950s the A level examination developed slowly but surely. New syllabuses were produced and the boards took ever greater care to standardise the marking of their Assistant Examiners. It was the establishment in the late 1950s of the Nuffield Science Teaching Project which led to the first major development. Initially, new O level and then, new A level science syllabuses and examinations were produced. A number of science teachers had come together under the umbrella of, what we now know as, the Association for Science Education to develop new syllabuses and eventually new schemes of examination. This work became supported by the Nuffield Foundation. A number of science teaching projects was established along principles imported from America. Full time staff were appointed to each project and the teams were housed firstly at the Foundation's Headquarters and later at The Centre for Science and Mathematics Education at Chelsea College. The Nuffield Science Teaching Projects were not simply new syllabuses,* they were complete curriculum packages with books for teachers, draft programmes, teaching materials, especially designed equipment with 8 mm film cassettes, pupils' workbooks, well presented information booklets, data books and, most importantly, new examinations. The Nuffield science teaching syllabuses were among the first to put an emphasis on higher order skills such as analysis, synthesis, comprehension and evaluation.

Once schools were freed from the necessity of entering a student for a prescribed group of examination subjects, competition between the boards began to develop. At first it was not extreme as the number of A level candidates was rising rapidly and many schools and colleges were teaching 18+ courses for the first time. Nevertheless, the decision in 1960 to permit the establishment of a further examination board, the Associated Examining Board, appears a little perverse. The board was established in the first instance to conduct A level examinations for the developing further education sector. However, its initially rather traditional syllabuses also proved extremely popular with the increasing numbers of comprehensive schools.

Changes were also taking place within the other GCE boards. As the 1960s proceeded they turned from being university dominated organisations to ones in which representatives of teachers' organisations had a controlling influence. The Secondary Schools Examination Council was replaced in the early 1960s by the Schools Council which had an institutional commitment to innovation. These two factors turned most of the examination boards from reactive to proactive organisations.

As the numbers of examination candidates increased, it became increasingly necessary for the examination boards to automate their procedures. One of the first aspects of their administration to be computerised was that of standardising examination marks and awarding grades. Prior to the introduction of computers most boards employed large numbers of people – often undergraduates – during the summer holidays to scale the marks of individual examiners and whole papers so that the pass and distinction standards could be scaled to the pass and distinction percentage marks were the agreed 40% and 75% respectively. The idea of using machines to scale marks was attractive. The first computer programmers and systems analysts instead proposed the idea of grades which could be equated

---

* For a description of the organisation of the Nuffield Science Teaching Projects see Waring (1979).

with nominal mark ranges. The small year-by-year variations in the standards of individual subjects could be accommodated by changing the grade boundaries; and so A level grades were born.

The first system of grades was introduced by a small number of boards on their own initiative (see Table 2). This was a system of nine numerical grades: grade 1 corresponded to marks of 75% and above, an A level distinction; grade 6 was the lowest grade of pass; grades 7 and 8 corresponded to the 'allowed ordinary' grade; and grade 9 was an out-and-out failure.*

Table 2 *A level grades 1960–63 and their relationship to marks*

summer 1951 – winter 1960 % marks		summer 1960 – winter 1963 grade
75 and over		1
70 – 74		2
60 – 69		3
55 – 59		4
50 – 54		5
40 – 49		6
	pass grades	
	fail grades	
30 – 39		7/8
under 30		9

In 1960 the SSEC agreed with the boards a common seven grade system which was introduced in the summer of 1963. Grade A was the highest grade of pass, grade E was the lowest grade of pass, below grade E there was a grade O corresponding to the allowed ordinary grade and the final grade was grade F indicating a fail. Each grade was tied to a typical percentage of candidates (see Table 3).

The use of percentages of the candidates in this way may well have been responsible for the common belief that A level examinations are norm-referenced. The SSEC proportions were, however, intended to apply to typical subjects only and were thus only to be used as a guide. The system remained in use until 1987, when a modified scheme was introduced by the Secondary Examinations Council. (See Chapter 1, and below, for details of the current system.)

The percentages were based on an idea of approximate thirds. The

---

* When the A Level examination was introduced in 1951 it was believed that some students would proceed straight to A Level and not take O Level en route – a process which was referred to as 'by-passing'. As a result, provision was made in the A level grade system for those students who having failed to reach A level standard would not thus have had the consolation of an earlier O level pass. Students who had just failed A level were awarded an O level pass at A level. In the event by-passing proved to be rare.

Table 3 *A level grades 1963–87 and their relationship to percentage of candidates*

grade	% of candidates	cumulative % of candidates
A	10	10
B	15	25
C	10	35
D	15	50
E	20	70
O	[15]	[85]
F	[15]	100
		[estimates]

top 35% of the candidates – those with grades A to C – were deemed to have 'good A level passes', the next 35% – grades D and E – to have 'bare passes', and the bottom 30% to have failed at advanced (A) level. The proportions of students awarded grade O – the 'allowed ordinary level pass' grade – seems to have varied from board to board. While some seem to have awarded the grade to a set proportion, others went to some lengths to achieve comparability with the O level pass standard.

The move corresponded with the abolition of the State Scholarship system and its replacement with special papers. Initially, a student had to gain a 'good A level pass', (i.e. a grade A, B or C) before a S paper result could be awarded. This idea was soon abandoned and any pass grade became sufficient.

The period up to the mid-1960s proved to be one of steady and significant change within the A level syllabuses and examinations. Nevertheless, the system remained largely traditional. Demand for the limited number of university places was high and most A level students still came from the independent and grammar school sixth forms. Pressures for change were building up and these surfaced in the second phase. More students were staying on and wishing to take less traditional combinations of subjects. Changes within the teaching profession, as a result of the Robbins report, had so far had very little effect upon A level examinations and A level teaching.

The latter days of the SSEC also saw the introduction of the Certificate of Secondary Education (CSE) examination. The examination was intended for about half of the secondary school children who did not take GCE O level, and who were therefore unlikely to take A level. The event is of relevance to the story of A level for two reasons. Firstly, the GCE boards were offered the opportunity to manage the new examination and they refused. As a result separate CSE boards were established on a regional basis. In the 1980s the GCE boards were amalgamated with the CSE boards to create the

GCSE examining groups – a process which put the viability of some of the former in doubt. The decision of the GCE boards not to take responsibility of the CSE examination must be seen as probably the greatest mistake they made. Secondly, the CSE examination came to make considerable use of teachers' assessments, often in association with mode 3 examinations. The use of teachers' assessments is still slowly diffusing into the advanced level examination.

18+ developments under the Schools Council (1964–1983)

With the establishment of the Schools Council the whole climate of syllabus and examination development changed. The period was marked by much discussion of the curriculum and possible changes to 16 and 18+ examinations. This is the period in which most of the abortive attempts to reform the structure of the A level examination took place. The more evolutionary changes, that did come to pass were mainly the result of the processes which had been set in train during the earlier phase of the examination and/or by the examination boards themselves.

Curriculum and examination development at A level continued pace. During the mid to late 1960s almost every major A level subject had its own curriculum project. Each reflected new thinking about the teaching of a subject or its role in the curriculum. Many of the early ones were sponsored by the Nuffield Foundation and later ones by the Schools Council itself, often working in association with other bodies. The curriculum development projects often created the need for new examination techniques to assess the skills that they had encouraged and this in turn led to the introduction of further project examinations. Many of the project examinations did indeed diffuse away but a core remain to this day.

The idea of objective testing – including multiple choice and short answer questions – was imported with the curriculum development projects from America. These ideas were also taken up by other subjects and thus led to a general improvement in the reliability of the A level examination. The validity of the assessment was also considered to be important. Therefore, instead of replacing existing methods of assessment, these new techniques were used to supplement the existing ones. The trend to more complex examination structures had begun.

New forms of practical work were also developed and these often used assessments by teachers. Acceptance of the idea of teacher assessment caused problems for some boards, whose traditions lay with mode 1 written papers. As described in Chapter 1, teacher assessment was already in use with the A level examination system but only for borderline cases. Gradually, however, the value of the technique was demonstrated both in the CSE and later in the GCE systems. Tensions between the desire to increase the validity of assessment, with minimum sacrifices in reliability, were eventually resolved and teacher assessment of practical work became an accepted concept. The issue was not fully resolved until the next phase of the evolution of A level when it was agreed that teachers' assessments could be made acceptably reliable if both pre-assessment standardisation and post-assessment moderation were employed. The Nuffield Science teaching projects differed in their moderation procedures from most other subjects in one important way; they used statistical moderation.

When syllabuses were revised and new material was included, old syllabus material was very seldom dropped. Therefore, as this phase of the development of the examination continued the demands on both students and teachers became greater and the latter saw their freedom to teach in their own way becoming restricted. To counter this trend, the examination boards responded by providing ever more advice to teachers about the approach to be adopted in their teaching, the particular examples to be included and other general help. As a result of all of these processes the syllabuses were becoming progressively larger.

There is some ambiguity in the concept of the curriculum development project and the project examination. The prime purpose of these projects was to update the teaching of the subjects generally by the process of permitting the concepts and 'improvements' developed within the project to diffuse into the teaching of the subject and the more traditional examinations offered by the boards. Quite quickly the examination boards' syllabuses came to adopt the more worthwhile and interesting parts of the innovations associated with the project. When special project examinations are established, however, this served in some cases to preserve the identity of the project. The existence of such an examination can also in some ways fossilise the project. Examination board syllabuses, with their two to three year cycle of development and improvement, could quickly absorb new ideas and consolidate them. The project with their associated books, films, tapes and other materials could not change as quickly without requiring quite unreasonable degrees of investment by the schools.

As the 1970s proceeded a process of specialisation also took place in which particular components of A level examinations came to use single methods of assessment. By 1980 almost all A level subjects used a wide variety of assessment techniques and gave the examination as a whole the characteristic which most distinguished it from North American and European 18+ examinations. Although they may be said to have started the process, the project examinations did not tend to follow the trend. When first introduced they tended to be slightly more complex than the traditional syllabuses available at the time but thereafter have remained fairly static. Nowadays, few of these project examinations still remain and those that have are mainly in the areas of mathematics, science and geography.

More importantly the processes of curriculum change led to a more informed teaching profession and this in turn fuelled the process of curriculum development. The level of qualification of teachers was rising: more teachers had post-graduate certificates of education, the Bachelor of Education (BEd) had been introduced and its value recognised; in the early 1970s the Open University had been established and its first graduates contained a very high proportion of teachers; lastly, most universities had established systems of further diplomas and higher degrees in education. Partly as a result of developments in America and partly because of initiatives in the UK, the processes of curriculum change had themselves become a subject of academic study. Curriculum studies became an important part of teachers' professional education.

Post-graduate, professional training and development was not restricted to the teaching profession. From the legislation introduced in the 1970s, many professional bodies representing engineers, scientists and other technically-based professions were receiving royal charters which in turn enabled them to award their members chartered status. Possession of a graduate qualification had not been for some time enough in itself to confer professional status. Membership of the relevant professional body was also needed and this depended on both proven experience and breadth of professional education. Requirements of the chartered institutes made demands upon the universities which in turn changed perspectives with respect to broad-based study. (So far the concept of chartered status has not been applied to teachers, although some achieve it through membership of other professional bodies.)

Changes within the examination boards continued throughout the 1960s and 1970s. University links were weakened, teacher control became greater but towards the end of the 1970s commercial pressures and competitions between boards necessitated their transition into businesses. Nevertheless, the boards continued to see themselves as part of an academic partnership with the teachers. Despite the increasing complexity of syllabuses in examinations, commercial competition between the boards necessitated increasing academic and financial efficiency. It was through the use of computers that the boards were able to introduce ever more elaborate procedures without corresponding increments in their staffing and examination fees.

One of the most important areas of development within this period was the establishment by the examination boards of research units. These were developed in response to several pressures. Firstly, there was a need to develop and evaluate the new assessment techniques. Secondly, the need of the GCE boards to organise comparability studies. Apparent differences in the proportions of candidates awarded particular A level grades in major subject areas had continued to be a frequent topic for media attention. The senior research officers of the GCE board came together to constitute the standing research advisory committee (SRAC) which advises the GCE Secretaries on the conduct of inter-board comparability studies and other technical matters concerned with the examination. From the mid-1960s onwards the GCE boards organised a rolling programme of comparability studies in the major O and A level subjects. Over the years a wide variety of attempts were made to assess inter-board comparability but, with the possible exception of the cross-moderation method, few were generally successful. Only a small number of cases of severity or leniency in individual board's syllabuses were identified and it may well be that such differences as existed were less than the measurement error of the methods employed. The programme of comparability studies did much to reassure the public, and much of the current understandings of the nature of A level standards emanates from this work. Full reports of those comparability studies conducted at both A and O level can be found in Bardell, Forrest and Shoesmith (1978), and Forrest and Shoesmith (1985).

Research was just one example of the way in which the GCE boards co-operated. Since the early 1950s (see Bruce, 1969) the Secretaries of the GCE boards had met regularly to discuss matters of common interest and to formulate common policies. As the 1970s progressed other groups were established to co-ordinate issues such as common timetables and computer matters. The boards also co-operated at the academic level; their joint work with the project examinations has already been described. They took entries for each others examinations and many informal arrangements over the sharing of papers, procedures and materials also developed.

By the end of the 1970s, it was clear that there were problems with the A level system. After a long period of uncritical innovation the system was beginning to be seen as unwieldy. In key subjects there were often large numbers of syllabuses and it became very difficult for users of the examination results – higher education and employers – to understand what the students had studied, what skills they were supposed to have acquired, and the meaning of the grades awarded. Some of the new subjects that had been introduced had very quickly earned their place in the sixth form curriculum – statistics, environmental studies, and computing are examples – and have made a significant contribution to the breadth and validity of the system as a whole. Conversely, some of the new subjects and syllabuses introduced had failed to attract viable numbers of candidates. On the credit side, the GCE system as a whole, had, through the introduction of AO levels, become more responsive to the needs of the new sixth formers and students in colleges of further education.

A second major problem with the A level examinations in particular was that of regression. The introduction of extra, usually poorly correlated, examination components causes the final marks for the examination to bunch around the mean mark. This became a particular problem in some arts subjects, especially in the essay papers, where it was difficult to persuade Assistant Examiners to use the full range of marks.* The answer was to begin to move GCE examinations in the direction of criterion referencing by providing mark criteria and, almost paradoxically, shorter mark ranges. In some subjects it also proved possible to grade work directly using criteria. The efforts to spread marks were generally successful and in many cases the arts subjects came to have more widely spread marks than, supposedly more objective subjects, such as chemistry.

18+ developments under the SEC (1983–1988)

This third phase of the evolution of A levels really begins in the spring of 1979 with the return to power of the Conservative Government. However, it was not until early in 1980, that its influence began to be felt. At the beginning of the 1980s concerns about the A level system were held by the Government and other sections of society. Firstly, the accountability and unnecessary complexity of the system was being criticised. Secondly, the relevance of the A level systems and many other aspects of secondary education to the commercial and industrial future of the UK were being questioned. The new Government stressed that Britain had a 'market driven' economy in which all sections of the social services, including education, would have to adopt more business-like methods. Competition was often introduced into what had previously been state monopolies. While such an approach to the organisation of their activities was not new

---

* The difficulties of making examiners use the full range of marks is illustrated by the following, apochryphal, marking scheme for English literature essays:

25 out of 25 – the impossible answer
24 out of 25 – Shakespeare's answer
23 out of 25 – the answer of the leading authority on the author
22 out of 25 – my head of department's answer
21 out of 25 – my answer
20 out of 25 – a good research student's answer
19 out of 25 – a good A level grade A student's answer

Meanwhile at the other end of the ability range. . . .

3 out of 25 – answer shows evidence that the student has read the correct book
2 out of 25 – the answer shows evidence that the student has read a book
1 out of 25 – there is a name on the paper

shaping the final form of the new GCSE examination. The introduction to the GCSE National Criteria (DES, 1985) emphasised that the new examination sought to make assessable the important aspects of subjects and not, as it had previously implied had been the case with the GCE O level and CSE examinations, make easily assessable things important. This spirit served to move the discussion of desirable features in examinations such as differentiation and discrimination further away from quantities (marks) and towards qualities (criteria). The GCSE thus first followed and secondly initiated some of the work which was taking place in the GCE A level system to improve the discrimination of that examination by the use of grade descriptions and mark criteria. Their introduction into the GCSE was on the grounds of accountability, a concept that is only just being applied to the advanced level system. The GCSE grade criteria did not, unfortunately, prove to be a success (Kingdon and Stobart, 1988).

The SEC's handling of GCSE developments was not perfect. Despite its efforts, syllabuses still proliferated. The effects of the GCSE upon the advanced level system were profound. Most important were the short-term effects that resulted from the loss of the traditional links between the 16+ and 18+ examination systems. In the final rush to approve the GCSE syllabuses, these links were lost. It was left to the advanced level system to respond by bridging the gap for GCSE students by short-term syllabus changes and advice to schools. More optimistically, the arrival in the sixth form of the first students who have passed through the GCSE system offers new opportunities for A level examinations. While the students, in the view of many, have improved and broader skills, their knowledge of what may be expected of them during the study of A level subjects is slightly reduced. It is obviously vital that the 16+ to 18+ links are re-established in the near future.

New curricular and administrative ideas were incorporated in the GCSE and, although many of these were paralleled by similar initiatives undertaken by the GCE boards themselves, it seems to be only a matter of time before similar concepts are incorporated into GCE advanced level examinations.

While the attention of the SEC was mainly focused upon 16+ matters, it organised a programme of A level scrutinies and vetted all 18+ syllabuses, both A and AS levels. The initiative for major 18+ developments tended to rest, however, with the GCE boards and with the Government directly.

The nature of the GCE boards research into examinations changed during the SEC period. The rolling programme of comparability studies was suspended after 1980 while two Oxford researchers, Cohen and Johnson, investigated the applicability of generalisability theory to comparability studies. Their work was in effect a comparability study of comparability studies. The findings of this work

(Johnson and Cohen, 1983) were inconclusive. The programme of comparability studies was not reinstituted on a regular basis although studies in A level English, mathematics and a few other subjects were conducted.

Towards the end of the 1980s the GCE boards' researchers gave greater attention to practicability and accountability in the examination system and some conducted research into the effects of the two new examinations – the GCSE and AS level – upon students, teachers, styles of teaching, school organisation and implications for local education authorities (NEEDS Project, 1988 and 1989).

The first of the successful initiatives to be introduced into A level examinations during the period of the SEC was the A level common core exercise. Conscious of the criticisms about the numbers of syllabuses in some subjects and their variety, the GCE boards had organised exercises to develop common cores in 11 GCE A level subjects. The purpose of the exercise was to standardise the elements of the content and examinations in the 11 subjects. The form of the core varied from common content in some subjects to common aims and objectives in others. In no case did they prescribe more than half of the A level syllabus. It was also hoped that the common cores would be an aid to the establishment of interboard comparability.

The GCE A level common cores were published in 1983 and, for two further subjects in 1987. They were gradually implemented thereafter. In all 13 subjects the cores created the necessity for individual boards to revise their syllabuses, although in some cases a mere restructuring was sufficient.

The common cores were criticised from the start for a lack of coherence. Certainly too much freedom had been given to the individual subject working parties and it is now difficult to identify the common features of the common cores. Gradually, and partly as a result of the common core exercise, the influence of the GCSE National Criteria, and partly as a result of natural processes of syllabus design, GCE syllabuses came to have clear statements of aims, of objectives, of methods of assessment, of the relationship between components, mirroring on an unofficial basis many of the aspects of the developing GCSE National Criteria.

Soon after its formation the Secondary Examinations Council had an opportunity to demonstrate its influence over the GCE boards. Whittacker and Forrest (1983) had drawn attention to what they believed were anomalies in the system of awarding A level grades which had been introduced in 1963. Grade C in particular was, they suggested, extremely narrow, just 10% of the students. As this grade represented the typical minimum for university entrance Whittacker and Forrest reasoned that there were causes for concern. Not all the boards agreed. Some took the view that grade C had become a recognised standard in its own right and it was therefore permissible to let the proportions of candidates awarded that grade vary from subject to subject, and if necessary from year to year. The SEC, however, took the initiative and organised groups of administrators and researchers from the boards to discuss the problem and investigate new procedures.

The resulting grade system was introduced in June 1987. Grades E, B and A were awarded as before but the emphasis was placed on the quality of students' work. Grades C, D and a new grade N (to replace the 'allowed ordinary' grade which would have become outdated with the introduction of the GCSE), were to be awarded using ranges of marks. The system was something of a 'camel' and involved features of all three previous systems of grades: proportions of candidates; quality of work; and ranges of marks. It must be seen as a compromise, with all that that implies.

It is very difficult indeed to decide what the overall effect of the new grading system actually was. Comparison of the boards' statistics for 1986 and 1987 suggests that the new grading system was only partly successful in its primary aim – that of increasing the proportion of candidates awarded grade C.

In addition to standardising the method of awarding grades, the SEC took the opportunity to impose a measure of standardisation on some of the boards' traditional variations in procedures. This latter course of action was partly justified by drawing attention to the very narrow mark ranges of A level grades in some subjects – a matter which was already being actively tackled by the GCE boards.

The period of the SEC was not one of innovation in assessment methods at 18+. There were however two developments, both of which arose mainly at 16+, which, if they were to be used widely at 18+, would have major implications for the examinations as a whole. The first is the modularisation of syllabuses and examinations, and the second the Technical and Vocational Education Initiative (TVEI).

As soon as the new system of awarding advanced level grades was agreed, the focus of the GCE boards quite naturally turned to investigating whether or not there were common principles for assessing the quality of work in A level subjects at the three grades (E, B and A). One of the later A level comparability studies (Kingdon et al., 1986), which had focused on A level English, had indicated that all boards were using similar marking criteria at key grades. The research officers of the boards began work in 14 subjects to investigate whether agreed common bases for marking and for grading could be developed. The exercise was termed the 'A level grade descriptions study'; the GCE boards were reluctant to endow this exercise with the apparent exactitude associated with use of the term criteria. This exercise built on the earlier 18+ mark criteria and 16+

grade criteria exercises and served to move 18+ examinations yet further in the direction of criterion referencing.

The division of syllabuses into modules was at first a convenient method of structuring them, especially if they contained options. Where the numbers or combinations of options were large it was proving expensive to produce and distribute the necessary examination papers. One of the ways of making the exercise manageable, that has been tried in some of the new GCSE syllabuses, was to link the option modules studied with specific sections of a larger examination paper. The idea of modularising advanced level syllabuses is slowly gaining ground and some schools, groups of schools, and examination boards have begun to explore the idea of end-of-module assessment and using modules from different syllabuses to make new 18+ combinations. Phased assessment of this sort might well assess quite different qualities from the traditional end-of-course examination. Therefore, the SEC took a cautious approach, and allowed only a limited number of trial schemes.

The Technical and Vocational Education Initiative was established not by the Department of Education and Science, but by the Manpower Services Commission, at about the same time as the SEC came into being. The aim of the initiative was to create technically and vocationally orientated courses, mainly at GCSE but also at advanced level; the attraction, from the schools' point of view was the unusually generous funding.

Fourteen TVEI trial projects started in 1983 and the first examinations were organised in 1985. These were typically for the GCSE and of the mode 3 form. All could be criticised for over-assessment. After the first trial examinations the scheme was opened up to all local education authorities and schools. Some 18+ schemes have been produced, but the overall impact of TVEI at that level must be judged to be small.

At the beginning of the 1980s there was considerable variation between the GCE boards in the extent to which they were computerised. Some were operating what were practically hand crafted operations. One or two still used hand drawn graphs to scale marks. Some boards used computers to support marking procedures and the remainder had automated their processes to the probable limit of the then-available technology. Almost all of the GCE boards have ended the 1980s having established their computer systems around fully integrated database systems. In the most advanced of these, links are made automatically between: incoming candidate entries; the papers that they will sit; the examiners to mark the papers; etc. The use of such computers had permitted the administration of ever more complex assessment techniques by facilitating the different types and greater quantities of data needed to question or confirm Chief Examiners' judgement of standard. The initial stimulus was the development of the GCSE and latterly the introduction of AS levels. Many of the new systems possess sufficient flexibility to be both administrative and research tools. New problems and situations can be modelled and many important 'what if' questions raised by Chief Examiners can be answered before or during the awards.

It would be wrong to give the impression that these sophisticated computers have made the examination boards more impersonal, quite the contrary. The procedures and statistics from their computers are used by the boards to support their Chief Examiners in the judgement of the quality of individual candidate's work. The modern database systems have also enabled far more information to be brought under the instant control of examination board officers answering telephone calls and otherwise dealing with queries raised by or about individual students. Lastly, it is important to stress that it is only through the use of such sophisticated computer techniques that it has been possible to keep the costs of the A level examination from rising in proportion to the complexity of the examination processes. The computers should thus be seen as an aid to greater accountability in both financial and technical terms.

The SEC's responsibilities did not extend to the systems of vocational qualifications taken in further education colleges. During the development of the GCSE some schools had also introduced such courses and it could be said that the vocational system had become a rival to GCSE and GCE examinations. The vocational systems of examinations were complex and little understood, by users and students. To solve this problem the National Council for Vocational Qualifications (NCVQ) was founded in 1986. The NCVQ's brief was two-fold. Firstly, it set out to improve vocational qualifications by anchoring them to agreed standards of occupational competence, and secondly, to establish a framework of National Vocational Qualifications (NVQ) which would facilitate access and progression, and would be understandable to users.

Several features of the work of the NCVQ are of interest in the context of advanced level examinations. The NVQ framework is based on a system of levels; these are skill- and competence-based, and partly criterion referenced. A system of credit transfer is also possible.

As when any new, and potentially rival, organisation is established, existing bodies are cautious. This was certainly the case in early contacts between the GCE boards and the NCVQ. The significance of the NCVQ ideas for the advanced level system, however, are considerable. There is some overlap in the candidatures of the two systems. Both represent major steps and the ladders of opportunity – albeit rather different ladders – that reach from the school to higher professional qualifications.

It was the Government's continuing desire to make the school system as a whole more accountable to employers, to local communities and to parents which led to the development of the National Curriculum. The 1988 Education Reform Act which paved the way for the National Curriculum and other innovations also necessitated the replacement of the SEC by a new body – the School Examinations and Assessment Council (SEAC) – with wider responsibilities and powers. The SCDC was, in effect, replaced by the National Curriculum Council (NCC).

Despite its power to influence the examination system the impact of the SEC at 18+ was not large. Of the two major initiatives within the 18+ sphere, both were directed by Government departments. The introduction of AS levels which was instituted directly by the Department of Education and Science, and the Welsh Office; the establishment of the Higginson Committee was undertaken by the Prime Minister's office. As already indicated above, other initiatives were undertaken by the GCE boards working either as individuals or collectively. The GCE advanced level system was also under attack from other directions and ended the SEC period slightly weakened. The International Baccalaureate examination had begun to make some in-roads into the prestige, if not the clientele, of GCE examinations, and the various forms of vocational education were also having their impact even in the GCSE age ranges.

The development of examinations and assessment under the SEAC

The introduction of the SEAC and NCC was more than a simple restructuring of the two previous organisations. Firstly, the responsibilities of the SEAC include the systems of vocational education qualifications offered by RSA, BTEC, CGLI etc. Secondly and more importantly, the ability of the SEAC to direct, and indeed, to limit the production of new syllabuses will be profound. Unlike its predecessors the SEAC has no obligation to approve new syllabuses unless the boards concerned are able to demonstrate the need for such syllabuses.

Work to develop a National Curriculum for England and Wales had begun in 1987. The Task Group on Assessment and Testing (DES, 1988d) was established under the chairmanship of Professor Paul Black of King's College. The TGAT committee reported in December 1987 and proposed a new and common model for the school curriculum 5 to 16. It included:

(a) *A system of core and foundation subjects.* The core is to be made up of mathematics, science and language (English or – for Welsh medium schools in Wales – Welsh as a first language). The foundation subjects are to be technology, history, geography, music, art and physical education, and modern languages. For English medium schools in Wales, Welsh will be taught as a second language.

(b) *A system of 10 levels of attainment.* These will reach from the attainment to be expected of typical children at the end of their first year of schooling (level 1), to the level of attainment to be expected of the most able GCSE students (grade A/level 10). The GCSE grades are being redefined to consolidate the links with the National Curriculum levels.

(c) Education 5 to 16 was divided into a number of key stages:
- Key Stage 1 – 5 to 7 year olds
- Key Stage 2 – 7 to 11 year olds
- Key Stage 3 – 11 to 14 year olds
- key stage 4 – 14 to 16 year olds.

The Key Stages correspond with the usual divisions of the English school system – infant school, junior school, non-specialist secondary work, and specialist secondary course (GCSE).

(d) Programmes of study for each subject are being issued for each of the Key Stages. Teachers will, nevertheless, retain the freedom over how to interpret and implement the programmes of study.

(e) Children's progress is to be measured by *teachers' assessments*, which will be undertaken concurrently with the teaching process; and, a system of *standard assessment tasks (SATs)* which will make an independent assessment of each child at the end of each key stage.

(f) Each subject is broken down into a series of hierarchical subdivisions: profile components; attainment targets; levels; and, statements of attainment (assessment criteria).

Teaching of the National Curriculum began in September of 1989 and assessment arrangements are being introduced from 1991 when the first unreported run (FUR) for Key Stage 1 will take place. SATs for other key stages and subjects will be introduced gradually thereafter.

Although work to develop the programmes of study and attainment targets for mathematics, science and English began almost at once, the implementation of the National Curriculum as a whole required the passing of the 1988 Education Reform Act. The probable effects of the introduction of the National Curriculum on the 18+ examination system are as yet unclear but are likely to be profound. The National Curriculum holds out the hope of bringing students with a broader subject base, plus more clearly defined skills and competencies in to GCE advanced level examination work, and at a younger age. The impact of Key Stage 4 and its relationship to the GCSE is as yet unclear.

Another provision of the Education Reform Act – the introduction of local management of schools – is likely to have implications for GCE advanced level examinations. School governors will take responsibility for school budgets and there are potential implications in this for a system which depends on examination fees.

Already the SEAC has been able to demonstrate its influence by continuing the systems of A level scrutinies and by monitoring the first AS level examinations. Very soon after its formation the Secretary of State asked the SEAC to conduct a review of examination provision for the 16 to 18 age group, incorporating the systems of vocational education. This work was to involve both the NCC and the NCVQ.

GCE advanced level examinations in 1990

Assessment techniques

The move to criterion-referenced assessment is not only established within 18+ examinations but also within the GCSE system and most significantly within the new National Curriculum. It is clear from current work at AS level (see Chapter 5) and from the ways in which the AS level syllabuses were received, that further work is likely to begin shortly on the establishment of common cores for A level possibly incorporating AS level work. The number of examination components is, in my view, unlikely to increase in the short term because of financial implications. It is likely however that the establishment of new common cores and the greater use of criterion referencing may well change quite radically the form of the individual components.

The curriculum

It now seems inevitable that the curriculum of the sixth form, whether for individuals or for sixth formers as a whole, is likely to become broader. However, unless new methods of organising sixth form courses are introduced and additional resources are provided this broadening of the sixth form curriculum may be constrained due to financial reasons.

Students

If the National Curriculum is to fulfil its promise it seems reasonable to expect that students arriving to take advanced level A and AS level courses will be better prepared and bring to their sixth form courses a wider spectrum of subjects with their inherent skills and experiences. As indicated above, the establishment of the National Curriculum may well serve to bring the brighter students earlier to GCE work. The growing breadth of the curriculum, the obvious desire of the SEAC and the NCC to establish vocational links may mean that students take a very much broader range of courses although it is unclear at the present time the degree to which some very specialist faculties in universities (mathematics, physical sciences and languages) may welcome such a development.

GCE boards

It seems inevitable that the number of GCE boards will decline over the next few years. Many have not yet recovered the financial investments that they made in the development of GCSE and AS level syllabuses. To begin now on a new round of 18+ developments and possible changes at GCSE due to the introduction of the National Curriculum may cripple them.

Reading between the lines of the DES, SEAC and NCC booklets, the GCE boards may move to a system of weak opposition in which only a limited number of the boards are able to offer syllabuses in particular subject areas.

The teachers

The National Curriculum and local management of schools are likely to put immense pressures upon teachers. However, if they are able to respond (indeed if the demands are reasonable), this may well be one of the major steps in turning teachers into true professionals. All of the recent assessment developments, be they from 5 to 16 or 16 to 18, have put new pressures on schools and teachers to develop better systems of management, of co-ordination of whole school policies, of assessment, and of intercurricular links. These developments will require not only large numbers of in-service (INSET) courses to meet the immediate needs of teachers but also a greater need for extended professional study.

Universities

With so many changes within the school system, and potentially within the GCE advanced level system, universities and higher education in general may also have to change. It is inconceivable that the sixth form system and 18+ examinations should be expected to respond to both innovative developments pre-16 years and a reluctance of higher education as a whole to respond. While there is much evidence for believing that many tutors in higher education would favour broader based entrance, some may be reluctant to do so if the breadth is achieved at the expense of specialisation that admission tutors may see as essential for advanced work in their faculties. The real test of the universities' commitment to a broader sixth form education will have to be demonstrated by the willingness of admission tutors to admit students with broader and less specialised qualifications.

FIVE

AS levels: a case study in broadening advanced levels

Introduction

The immediate origins of AS level examinations lie in the consultative document *Examinations 16–18* issued by the Secretaries of State for Education and Science, and for Wales (DES, 1980b). The Secretaries of State reaffirmed their beliefs in contemporary A levels as: standards of excellence; the foundation of degree courses; and, the best means of selection for higher education. They proposed that A levels would continue for the foreseeable future, but expressed concerns about the degree of specialisation that the pursuit of good A level results and entrance to higher education tended to engender. Their proposed solution was the establishment of a new intermediate level examination to be taken alongside A levels – the new examination to require perhaps half the teaching and study time over two years. The purpose of the new examination would be to broaden a student's studies by allowing him or her to replace one or more of their A level subjects by a larger number of the 'intermediate' level courses. The idea received a positive, but guarded, response from most sectors of education and employment.

A further consultation document entitled *AS levels* was published by the Secretaries of State (DES 1984). This contained further details of the proposed examination, now renamed the 'advanced supplementary level'. The new examination was to be taught alongside A levels rather than serve as a stepping stone between 16+ and 18+ examinations as the term 'intermediate' might seem to imply. Once again the approach to the broadening of the sixth form curriculum contained in the AS proposals was to offer students the opportunity to study half credit courses for examination at 18+.

The value of the specialist sixth form curriculum, with AS levels as a broadening element, was proposed. It was assumed that two A levels would continue to be the basis of entrance to degree courses, and one for admission to higher national certificate courses. The innovatory, and most challenging, feature of AS levels was that, while they would require only half the teaching and study time, they would still maintain the same degree of academic rigour as full A levels. It was also suggested that the implementation of AS levels could be achieved without the provision of extra teaching resources!

As described in the 1984 booklet, AS levels were presented as something of a political panacea – a broader curriculum without any reduction in standards *and* all with no extra resources. Nevertheless, in their reactions to the AS level proposals, institutions of higher education and employers indicated their willingness to accept the new qualification, and schools and colleges their willingness to introduce the necessary courses. The result of the consultation exercise was a guarded but generally positive reaction to the concept of an advanced supplementary level examination. Warnings were sounded by the examination boards' syllabus developers and research staff about relative A and AS level standards, and by schools about the idea of co-teaching. Nevertheless, these sets of concerns were not allowed to dampen the generally favourable response to the AS level concept. The document 'AS Levels' became the blueprint – albeit a limited one – for the development of the new examination.

The go-ahead to develop the new AS level examination was given in the document *Better Schools* (DES, 1986a). It was clear that the proposals made in *AS levels* the previous year had been modified in the light of reactions received and now provided a basis from which the implementation of the examination could begin. Some features of the examination were subsequently to evolve further as the GCE boards developed syllabuses and submitted them for approval to the Secondary Examinations Council. Outline details of how the principles of the new examination evolved during the development and approval of the first AS level syllabuses can be found in the Council's annual reports.

Most students, their parents, school and college staffs gained their first knowledge of the AS level examination from a series of leaflets issued by the Department of Education and Science (DES, 1986a, 1987a, and 1986b). These were entitled *Broadening Your A Level Studies: A Guide for Schools and Colleges* (1986 and 1987); and *A Guide for Students and Parents* (1986). They became known as the 'blue, green and orange waterproof leaflets' respectively, being issued with a high gloss coating that proved to be remarkably resistant to hot staffroom coffee. Other leaflets and booklets followed.

Future historians may be somewhat surprised at the way in which the features of the AS level examination were presented as original and were so inadequately discussed. They might even wonder why the AS concept could not have been implemented before. There may be two reasons why AS levels succeeded when similar earlier pro posals had failed. Firstly, the development was timely. There was a general agreement about the need for a broadening of the sixth form curriculum and there was a climate of examination innovation. Many people with an interest in 18+ examinations were keen to see the sort of efforts and resources, as had been necessary to develop the GCSE, put behind examinations at the higher level. Secondly, an unusual feature of the development and implementation of AS levels has been the DES's active marketing of the new examination. The then Secretary of State for Education and Science, Kenneth Baker, made a personal endorsement of AS levels. If political support of this sort was a guarantee of success, then AS levels had a rosy future.

The initial thinking behind AS levels was inadequate. During the development of AS level syllabuses and examinations, and during the first two years of their teaching, problems arose in connection with the relationships between A and AS level syllabuses; the definition of AS level standards; and the implementation of AS level courses.

This chapter considers two aspects of the introduction of the AS level examination. Firstly, the proposed features of the examination are reviewed and the support for the implementation of the examination discussed. Secondly, the practical implications for the examination boards and for teachers are considered. The experiences gained from the first examination of AS levels in 1989 are incorporated in the continuing story of advanced level given in the next chapter.

AS features

Broadening advanced level studies

The AS level proposals were designed to achieve a broader curriculum in two ways. Firstly, students were able to continue more of the subjects that they had studied to 16+, or start new ones. Secondly, the HSC and major/minor/general proposals for 'supporting' and 'contrasting' subjects were resurrected. Courses were to be broadened by the addition of new subjects from both outside and within the students' specialist areas – these are termed 'contrasting' and 'complementary' subject combinations respectively. The green leaflet offered English for science students, or mathematics for humanities students as illustrations of the former, with design and technology for scientists as an example of the latter. Some syllabuses were designed with contrasting or complementary roles in mind, e.g. 'Contemporary French' or 'Mathematics with Applications (complementary)'.

The idea was also proposed that AS levels could be introduced without the necessity of additional examining resources by the use of common A/AS level components. This was considered to be an aid to the 'co-teaching' of the two groups of students. The practical implications of these ideas were not developed and led to later problems.

Target population

AS levels (DES, 1984) stated clearly that the target population for the new examination was intended to be full time, two year, A level students. The paper also suggested that the examination could also serve the needs of other groups – especially mature students. *Better Schools* (DES, 1986a) described the target population as 'the brightest 17 to 18 year olds' and expressed the hope that wider choice of subjects would lead to more enjoyable courses. Two AS levels were to be considered in all respects – demand, teaching/study time and value – equivalent to an A level.

AS level subjects

It was initially proposed that AS level courses would be developed in all subjects for which there was sufficient demand. Nevertheless mathematics, physics, chemistry, biology, technology, modern languages (French, German, Welsh), history and geography were suggested as suitable for the first round, and general studies, economics, computer studies, and design and technology for the second. Following the consultation process, mathematics, English, modern languages, design and technology, and general studies were identified as the priorities for the development of AS level syllabuses and were sponsored by the Government.

AS level grades

AS level syllabuses were to lead to the same seven point grade system introduced in 1987 for A levels. Grades A to E were to represent passes – A being the highest – Grade N to represent a near miss and Grade U an unclassified performance. Even if A and AS level syllabuses were to share common components, sections or questions, there was to be no possibility of any AS level grades being awarded for a poor performance on an A level examination. This policy represents a clear difference from the main and subsidiary level system used in the Higher School Certificate.

It was suggested, rather simplistically, in *AS levels* that common examination components might be a means of saving resources while assisting in the achievement of comparability between A and AS level syllabuses. The same idea has been extended to common elements of the two levels.

Questions arose immediately about whether two AS levels would require more work than one A level and whether contrasting subject combinations might prove more difficult than complementary ones. The whole ethos of the AS level proposals was to encourage the use of contrasting subjects. Should it subsequently be found that contrasting A level subjects were indeed more difficult then this would need to be compensated for in some way; perhaps through more favourable higher education admission requirements.

Administrative arrangements

AS levels (DES, 1984) proposed that the development of AS levels should be placed in the hands of the GCE Boards of England and Wales – if the new level was to relate to A levels it is difficult to anticipate in what other hands it might have been placed. In practice, only six boards, or groups of boards, published AS level syllabuses for the first examination in 1989:

- AEB
- COSSEC (a consortium of Cambridge, Oxford & Cambridge and SUJB)
- JMB
- London
- Oxford
- WJEC

(Northern Ireland published their first AS level syllabuses in 1988 for examination two years later.)

As with the other GCE examinations, the entry arrangements were to be kept flexible. The blue leaflet stated that AS levels could be taken in one year, and that it was possible to study any number of AS level subjects – shades of the earlier major/minor/general and N and F proposals. It was also anticipated that syllabuses based on former AO levels might become the basis of (one year) AS level courses. It had become the tradition for the better mathematics students to proceed from O, to AO, to A level mathematics, and even to A level further or higher mathematics. With AO levels being discontinued after 1988, it seemed likely that AS level mathematics would become the new stepping stone to higher attainment in the subject. Other AS level subjects also seemed likely to become used in this way.

Higher education and employment

Responses by institutions of higher education to the document *AS levels* indicated that they considered that the proposed examination was the best (and perhaps the only) means of broadening sixth form studies that was likely to prove acceptable to all parties. The same set of proposals had called on higher education bodies to confirm their support for a broader range of subjects and in the blue leaflet it was confidently stated that the universities and polytechnics would willingly modify their entrance requirements to recognise students with AS level results. SCUE – the universities' Standing Council on University Entrance – did much to promote the idea of AS levels and published statements by the universities expressing support for the new examination. Almost all universities, polytechnics and colleges of higher education began at once to revise their entrance requirements. These requirements come in two forms: general and faculty. Changing the first was easy; making changes to the latter less so, especially if students took contrasting combinations of subjects.

There are still some doubts, however, that the purposes of the new examination are fully understood by all admissions tutors. It is this fear, above all other factors, that is likely to result in the schools and colleges, and their students, continuing to have a toe-in-the-water approach to AS levels.

The Government has also taken strenuous steps to encourage major employers and professional bodies to endorse the AS level examination. The Civil Service has also undertaken to revise its admission procedures. The schools, students and parents are likely, however, to remain cautious for some time to come.

Demands upon teachers

In the initial proposals it appeared that the demands upon teachers of AS levels would be considerable. Firstly, *AS levels* (DES, 1984) proposed the idea of A and AS level 'co-teaching' but in the blue document this concept was largely rethought and described as 'not ideal'. Secondly, AS levels could be seen as a reaction against non-examined liberal education courses. The new examination would inevitably have to take some of the time and resources that had previously been allocated to non-examination enrichment courses. Non-examined courses were not, it was currently believed, valued by the Government. Some teachers saw the move from non-examined to examined time as regrettable. Thirdly, sixth form teachers felt that they were under unreasonable pressure to start AS level courses. Establishing such courses was not necessarily an easy matter. Teachers often had to convince their colleagues, parents, students and local employers.

Take up

The Secretary of State's stated hope was that 95% of all schools and colleges that taught A levels would have introduced at least two AS level courses by 1990. This is a surprisingly modest aim and would not, unless large numbers of students could be persuaded to take-up the AS levels offered, produce a significant broadening of the 18+ curriculum.

The rationale of AS levels

The case for broadening the sixth form curriculum in general, and its achievement through AS levels in particular, was not well made. Apart from references to desirable qualities that it was thought might result from AS level courses, the argument seldom rose above the 'more is better' level. The second strand of the broadening strategy – the use of contrasting subjects – was illustrated but otherwise poorly developed. Students, their parents, and teachers could be forgiven for believing that contrasting subject combinations would be more difficult, it remained unclear how such extra efforts might be rewarded. The concept of co-teaching was considered to be potentially unworkable and those with knowledge of assessment techniques expressed concerns about the equality of AS and A level standards, and their achievement via common elements. Nevertheless these reservations were not permitted to hinder the implementation of AS levels.

One particular factor that has bedevilled the development of AS levels and discussion of their impact on the sixth form curriculum, has been the lack of suitable models with which to describe and evaluate the effects of broadening. The model used to explain AS levels was a particularly simple one.

In the attempt to explain both the intended relationships between A and AS levels, and the relationship between depth and breadth of study, the Department of Education and Science has made use of an analogy of subjects as triangles. (See Figure 2)

The model was essentially a spatial one. In other sections of the DES literature on A and AS level developments, it was being suggested that depth and breadth can be considered as independent dimensions of attainment. It was thought that it was possible to develop AS level syllabuses which have the same depth of study as A levels but require only half the teaching time. In Figure 2 the bases of the triangles represent the breadth of study; the height of the triangles the depth of study and the degree of academic rigour. The area of the triangles are equated to the overall demands that the individual syllabuses make. Looking at the two AS level syllabuses represented on the right hand side of Figure 2 it can be noticed that there is some overlap between them. It is presumed that this represents the degree of common skills, knowledge and/or content inherent between pairs of AS level subjects. This overlap will be larger in the case of cognate subjects. The symbolism of the balance is well chosen for publicity purposes, but does it offer promises that may not be deliverable?

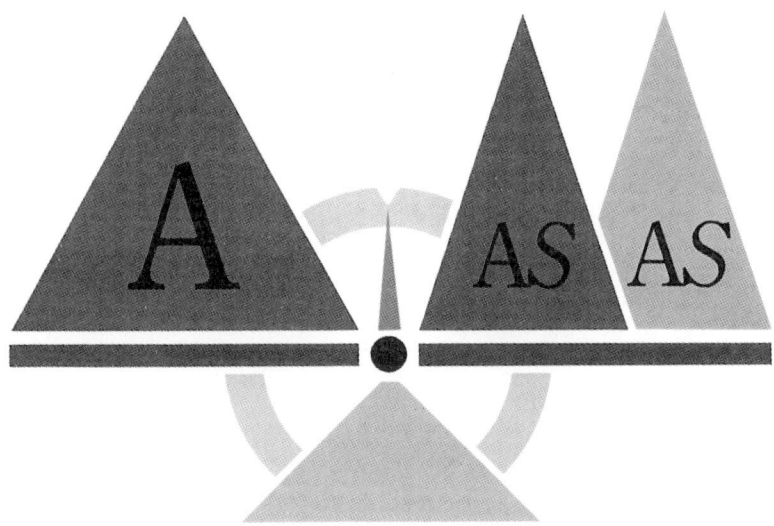

Figure 2   *The relationship between A and AS levels (DES, 1987a)*

It is possible to stretch the model to draw further points. Firstly, it can be noted that the base of the A level triangle is no larger than the joint bases of the two AS levels. This may well imply that merely to replace one A with two AS levels might not of itself have a broadening effect. It is the degree of 'curricular distance' between two AS levels that may be the true measure of broadening. Secondly, the area of the combined AS triangles is slightly larger than that of the A level. While this is probably unintentional in the context from which the diagram comes, it hints at the idea that the study of two AS levels might require more than the study of one A level. As the curricular distance between two AS levels increases, the overlap will decrease and the total demands increase. Thirdly, the triangles on both sides of the balance are apparently solid. No attempt has been made to illustrate the possibility of lighter syllabus structures. Lastly, because of their narrower bases, the AS level triangles have steeper sides. Does this imply that AS levels are constructed of slightly different materials, or that they have some form of internal cross bracing? Could it be that without these features, AS levels risk academic subsidence?

The SEC (1986) warned against taking the spatial model too far. Nevertheless, no other simple model so far exists (and more complex, and mathematical ones are probably inappropriate in this case).

AS level implementation: practical problems for the examination boards and schools

The response of the GCE Advanced Level examination boards to the idea of the AS level examination was enthusiastic. The boards had long agreed with the need to broaden the sixth form curriculum and generally considered the proposals as a practical way of doing so. Nevertheless, there was a major problem: namely, how syllabuses could be constructed that required half the teaching and study time while still retaining the same intellectual rigour. Initially, the issue was swept aside (perhaps because of fear that to draw too much attention to it might be interpreted as a luke warm response to the proposals as a whole).

Very early on in the discussions between the Department of Education and Science, the Secondary Examinations Council and the GCE boards, the idea was proposed on the Government's side that AS levels should only be developed in certain subject areas and that individual GCE boards might be given responsibility for developing the 'official' AS level syllabus in a particular subject. This proposal was very much in line with the Government's consistent desire to reduce the number of syllabus titles at A level. The idea, however, did not find favour with the GCE boards; each feared that boards sponsored to develop the AS level syllabus might then come to have a dominating position within the A level market for the same subject. Therefore, almost all boards set-off to develop syllabuses in a very wide range of subjects and in the event very few were actually sponsored. Even when they were, the degree of sponsorship tended to fall short of the real costs of syllabus development and implementation.

The boards set about the development of AS level syllabuses in a variety of ways and a number of distinctive approaches can be identified.

(a) Some boards took the suggestion in the 1984 document *AS levels* literally, that AS levels could be developed without the need for extra examining resources and could use some of the examination components from the existing A level. This idea necessitated the creation of AS levels syllabuses as part – usually more than half – of existing A level syllabuses. Some boards used this approach and took the opportunity to restructure their A level syllabuses so that the relationship, both for examiners and for teachers, between the A and AS level syllabuses became clearer. Many boards would undoubtedly have liked to have taken the opportunity to revise, rather than just restructure, their A level syllabuses, but with the concurrent pressures of GCSE syllabus development for 1988, few were able to do so in more than one or two subjects.

Better Schools (DES, 1986a) took this model a stage further and proposed the relationship that AS levels should be based on the A level common cores, where they existed. However, those boards that set out to develop AS level syllabuses in this way ran into immediate difficulties. The A level common cores had not been developed as free-standing syllabuses in their own right. They had, as the name implied, been developed to be common areas of content, skills, and aims which were intended to exist within the wider A level syllabus framework. Therefore, AS level syllabuses designed in this way tended to lack coherence. This became a major problem when the draft syllabuses were brought before the 18+ Committees of the SEC for approval, and many were initially rejected for this reason.

(b) In some instances individual GCE boards decided to build their AS level syllabuses by using a mixture of components from the A level examination with other components specially written for the AS level. Still others decided to use some of the sections of the A level papers as part of the AS level examination. The value of this approach must vary from one syllabus to another: the issue is once again that of coherence. The use of common A and AS level papers or sections, even if they represent only a subset of the AS level examination, still seems to infer a spurious comparability.

(c) A small number of boards decided to re-think the principles underlying the A level syllabuses in order to facilitate AS level developments. They had already been working towards the modularisation of their A level syllabuses, although this was seldom extended beyond the identification of one or more modules with a particular component of the examination. Where such modularisation was already being contemplated it was easier to make the distinction between the AS and non-AS level sections of the A level syllabuses. While this approach would obviously be of help to teachers trying to co-teach A and AS level groups, it suffered from the problem that AS level was still being seen as a sub-set of A level rather than something of a distinct, but equal, academic nature.

(d) At least one GCE board decided to take a completely different approach to the development of AS level syllabuses. Conscious of the issues of coherence and comparability that might result from building AS level syllabuses which used some or all of the A level components, the board took the opportunity to devise completely free-standing AS level syllabuses.

This individual board – or in some cases its subject advisory panels – reasoned that, in effect, to take a sharp knife to an A level syllabus and to pare it down might not be the most appropriate approach to the development of an examination of equal difficulty. For example, some historians reasoned that as the usual pattern for A level history syllabuses was to study two or more periods of history, each serving as a contrast for the other, simply to study one might be to miss the value of the subject as a whole. A more coherent syllabus might be devised by providing something which was free-standing and achieved its own internal contrasts − between times or countries − in other ways. The degree to which common A and AS level teaching could be contemplated using such syllabuses would vary, of course, with the examples of the two levels used.

(e) Almost all boards were keen to maintain the link that AO levels had represented as steps between 16+ and 18+ examinations in some subjects. Therefore, with the demise of the AO level examination almost all boards set about the development of AS syllabuses to bridge the gap. This was seen to be particularly important in the area of mathematics where able students had traditionally taken O level a year early and studied AO level mathematics in the fifth form, or had studied both O and AO levels concurrently and taken them together in the fifth form. The development of an appropriate AS level would enable the step to be re-established between 16+ examinations (the GCSE) and A level. The possibility also existed, of course, that an AS level developed in this way might also serve the needs of other students in the sixth form who, rather than wishing to specialise in mathematics might use it in a complimentary or contrasting subject. In the event, however, syllabuses in mathematics proliferated and special 'contrasting' and 'complementary' versions appeared.

There is a danger inherent in equating an AS level with one of the former AO levels. As will be reasoned in the next section of this chapter, the standards of the AS level examination, if they are to be equivalent to A level, are very different indeed from those of the old AO.

(f) The London GCE board in response to requests from a school − the Ridgeway School, Swindon − agreed to take the process of modularisation of A and AS level syllabuses a step further by developing the idea of end of module assessment. (See Axon 1989.) Six modules were to be studied for A level and three, in certain permitted combinations, for AS level. Organisation of 18+ examinations in this way appears to offer a very straightforward solution to the problem of syllabus design, joint examinations and common teaching. It involves, however, a departure from the pattern of a final end-of-course examination and thus is different in a number of significant (and little understood) ways from the existing models. The Ridgeway Scheme will be discussed in greater detail in the next section. The Higginson Report (DES, 1988c) endorsed the concept of modularisation but it is unclear as to whether end-of-course, or end-of-module assessment was being implied.

Syllabus issues

The brief given to the examination boards to maintain standards, was a tall one. The boards also had to be aware that some schools might well be trying to implement AS levels without extra resources and be contemplating common A and AS level teaching. Such factors could not, of course, influence standards but did necessitate clear statements of the connections between the AS and any A level syllabuses.

The SEC Annual Reports contain the only discussions of the technical aspects of AS syllabuses to arise during their development. The Council's staff were under no illusions about the difficulties that would have to be addressed if workable syllabuses were to be produced. In the 1985/6 report they regretted the lack of operational criteria but it was not clear whether they were referring to the need for clear guidelines with which to assess syllabuses – the GCSE National Criteria for example – or something more directly related to grades and outcomes, and along the lines of the GCSE draft grade criteria.

Underlying the whole process of AS level syllabus development is the concept of maintaining academic standards at 18+ – something that everyone supports but very few, even those directly involved, can define or provide suitable examples. The SEC has reasoned that if content could be meaningfully halved and other requirements kept the same, then AS levels would indeed become half A levels. Things are rarely, however, that simple.

Nevertheless, it seems reasonable to believe that coherent divisions of A level syllabuses could be achieved, e.g. the assessment of only three skills in an AS level modern language – listening, reading and speaking – rather than the usual four for A level. Such an AS level syllabus would also serve quite different purposes and, therefore, might also attract new groups of candidates to GCE examinations at 18+.

Developing strategies for the teaching of A and AS level courses in the sixth form

As soon as the teaching of the first AS level syllabuses began in September 1989, the GCE boards and the Department of Education and Science were very anxious to assess the take-up of individual syllabuses and the ways in which they had been taught in schools. Several surveys were organised and the following description is based mainly on one undertaken by the NEEDS Project (New Examinations, Evaluation and Development in Schools). This was organised jointly by the Institute of Education University of London, (initially) the Centre for Applied Research in Education, University of East Anglia, the University of London School Examinations Board, and the London East Anglian Group for GCE examinations.

The project which is still in operation at the time of writing, is considering the effect of the implementation of the GCSE and AS level examinations upon students, teachers, styles of teaching, and school organisation. The first survey of AS level developments (NEEDS, 1988) took place just before Christmas of 1987, only three months after the teaching of the first AS level syllabuses began. At that time it appears that only one tenth of the centres registered with the London board had actually implemented AS level courses. The number of syllabuses being offered by each school or college varied considerably, the commonest number being one and the highest ten. The average was two syllabuses per school or college. Not all of the syllabuses on offer had attracted students and from the comments of the respondents this was thought to reflect uncertainties about the standard of the examination, about the attitudes of universities to AS levels, and possibly about the future of examination as a whole caused by the recent establishment of the Higginson Committee. Nevertheless, at least seven different approaches to the teaching of AS level courses were identified.

1 Vertical divisions of A level syllabuses
In the establishment of AS level courses a large proportion of the schools and colleges had followed the ideas expressed in the 1984 document, *AS levels*, proposals and were attempting to teach new courses without extra teaching resources. From the NEEDS survey it was clear that the typical provision for A level students was some eight periods per week and that AS level students were attending half this number. In a minority of schools and colleges that were implementing this strategy the AS level students had one, or exceptionally two, periods per week on their own.

The success of this strategy must depend largely on the structure and content of the A and AS level syllabuses concerned. Not all A level syllabuses are easily devisable in this way and this approach may, in the long term, have to be restricted to those A and AS level syllabuses where the relationships between them are clearly stated. The vertical division of A level syllabuses could become an acceptable long term model if both sets of syllabuses were revised with co-teaching in mind.

Not surprisingly some of the schools and colleges that were attempting to adopt these methods were experiencing problems. One, from County Durham, was actually using an A level syllabus from one board together with an AS level syllabus from another in an attempt to make a suitable match between the two courses.

2 Horizontal divisions of A level syllabuses

The first NEEDS study indicated that the most popular model for the implementation of AS levels was for the school to set aside blocks of time – consecutive days or weeks – when A and AS level students could work together with occasional periods when the AS level students would be taught on their own. Initially the NEEDS researchers termed this strategy 'the box and cox method' but it is, of course, a *de facto* modularisation of the A and AS level syllabuses.

The method had certain inherent difficulties. Firstly, the distinction between what should be taught to both groups of students and what should be taught to A level students alone is a difficult one. Secondly such an approach may well lead to fragmentation of the AS level course and this could in turn effect both the attitudes and performances of the students concerned. It must be remembered that the AS level students may not always be those with the greatest motivation or positive attitudes towards the study of the subject. Thirdly, some schools and colleges had attempted to elaborate this idea and to teach the same students more than one AS level in the same timetable periods. The students were required to alternate between blocks of, say, history and French. Co-ordinating the timing of teaching of different subjects in this way was proving very difficult. The procedure could work, but required a very high degree of both academic planning and co-operation between departments.

Generally the concept of the horizontal division of a subject into common A and AS levels and A level only blocks has proved very difficult and some schools and colleges have actually had to withdraw AS level courses as a result. When the NEEDS researchers collected data for the second study in October and November 1988 (NEEDS, 1989) this method of organisation had declined considerably in popularity.

3 Separate A and AS level courses

Contrary to the original concept of the AS level examination, some schools and colleges had actually established separate courses for A and AS level students. These tended to be either those schools and colleges which were large, and therefore had the necessary resources, or those who had selected free-standing AS levels where common teaching, either of a vertical or horizontal form, was not appropriate.

4 AS levels in the first year – A level in the second

From the earliest studies it was quite clear that some schools proposed to teach AS level syllabuses in the first year with students then having the option of proceeding to an A level in the second. (This strategy has shades of the Q and F proposals of the mid-1960s.) Except perhaps in the area of mathematics, this idea is contrary to the spirit of the AS level examination which envisaged a two year course leading to A level. Nevertheless, study of AS level courses in one year is not precluded.

There are some dangers in this approach. Some schools and colleges may fail to have appreciated that the AS level examination is not a direct replacement for AO. Nor does it represent a standard half-way between that of 16+ and 18+ examinations. AS level syllabuses have been designed and AS level standards will be set with the assumption: that the students will have studied for a two year course, in effect five and a bit terms of study; that they will have had half the teaching time of an A level, say four periods per week; that they have the maturity of 18 year olds; and that they are taking other 18+ courses. Preparation for the AO level examination on the other hand tended to be for two and a bit terms. Except in mathematics, AO students did not typically have as many as four periods a week over two years, nor were AO students the most able. Officially, the standards of AO level were quite firmly equated with those of O level.

5 A common start to the A and AS level courses

Before the GCE O and A level achieved the complexity that they have now and before the GCE boards had agreed to co-operate over such matters as common timetabling, many schools found themselves with quite long periods of time between the end of the O level examinations and the beginning of the summer holidays. Many took the opportunity to induct their O level students into the sixth form and to commence A level studies – some even reported that they were able to teach a substantial proportion of the first half term's work before the end of the school year. However, with the rise of comprehensive education and the extension of the examination period the practice fell into disuse and sixth form induction procedures came to concentrate more on approaches to sixth form work in general rather than work in individual subjects.

The introduction of the AS level examination, presented sixth form tutors, not only with the problems of explaining the subject, and approaches to sixth form work, but also with the need to explain the differences between the A and AS examinations. This problem has been compounded by the introduction of the GCSE. O level examinations had been able to provide students with a flavour of what the subject would be like at the sixth form, i.e. they were end-on to sixth form courses. The same is not true of the GCSE and as a result many schools and colleges have found themselves with the need to start more elaborate induction procedures. The solution being tried by two of the centres that responded to the NEEDS questionnaire was to institute a common start to sixth form work, involving either the reintroduction of the period after 16+ examinations and before the end of the school term or a common start in September. Differentiation into A and AS level courses would then follow. In the school and college which had instituted a common start to two year A and AS level courses – whether through strategies two or five – found that students that had begun with the intention of taking AS level courses tended to up-grade themselves to the full A level. Contrary to what might have been expected, at the time of writing there has been very little evidence to suggest that students who started A level courses have 'dropped down' and converted to AS level courses – rather the reverse.

6 The use of AS levels to maintain or develop the width of sixth form provision

Some schools visited were clearly using the AS level examination as an opportunity to develop or maintain the width of their sixth form curriculum. Some were using the examination as an opportunity to introduce new subjects into the sixth form, in many instances as part of a deliberate policy of providing 'contrasting' courses. In some schools the width of the sixth form provision was actually under threat and due to unpopularity, staffing difficulties or falling roles, some A level courses were having problems of viability. The introduction of an AS level offered an opportunity both to retain the subject of the sixth form curriculum and hopefully to stimulate additional interest in years to come.

7 Modular A and AS level courses

A number of schools, colleges and consortia of schools and colleges decided to develop their own A and AS level courses frequently based on principles derived from the Technical and Vocational Education Initiative (TVEI). Not all of these developments have actually received immediate blessing from the SEC which appeared to be approaching the whole concept of modular courses at 18+ with some caution, and the idea of courses involving integrated or general studies at 18+ with extreme caution.

Probably the only A and AS level scheme dealing with the main stream sixth form subjects is the one proposed by the Ridgeway School, Swindon and which is outlined above. Syllabuses were developed and teaching commenced in June 1987 with seven subjects: biology; geography; history; English; economics; religious studies;

and French. Some of these syllabuses have been developed entirely by the staff of the school and some were the result of the 'modularisation' of London Board syllabuses. The scheme received outline approval by the then SEC and two cohorts of students were allowed to start in September 1987 and 1988 respectively. During the academic year 1988/89 the experiences of the staff and the examination board in working with the first students were considered by the SEAC and outline approval was given for the scheme to be extended to between 10 and 15 other centres and some 250 to 300 students in each subject. Individual subject syllabuses are being considered by the SEAC 18+ subject committees at the time of writing.

The Ridgeway school year has been divided into six blocks so that end of module assessments for individual subjects, all take place in the same weeks and interchange between AS level subjects is possible. The end of module assessments incorporate more than the usual variety of extended essays, practical work, field work and orals common with more traditional examination schemes. Two points follow from this. Firstly, by using such a wide range of techniques it may at first sight be thought that the Ridgeway scheme is over assessing its students. Secondly, and in part explanation of the first point, the scheme is blurring the distinction between end-of-module assessments and techniques which are traditionally used as part of sixth form teaching. As a result, the combined A and AS level assessment incorporate a very high proportion of what in other schemes would be termed 'class-work'.

At the time of writing the London Board and the SEAC are evaluating the results from the first Ridgeway awards of A and AS level grades. Initial take-up from within the school was necessarily limited and especially so with respect to AS level courses. It is likely to be some years, however, before the success of this scheme can be fully understood. Once again the pattern has been for some students to begin an AS level course and then to up-grade their studies after the first module.

The whole process of modularisation – if it is to be anything other than a division of the syllabus into parts – opens up new areas which are yet largely unexplored and therefore little understood. The policy of the SEAC in proceeding cautiously with respect to the Ridgeway and similar schemes therefore appears fully justified. The great fear might be that structuring courses in this way, particularly if end-of-module examinations are used, might actually prejudice standards by making them either too easy, in which case they would put other students at a disadvantage if the converse were to apply, the Ridgeway students themselves might be at a disadvantage. The Ridgeway scheme has raised two issues of fairness: the need for new awarding procedures and the need to extend the traditions of advanced level examinations in order to respond to the needs of individual students.

One approach to modular A and AS level awards, that seems to be suggested by the AS level proposals, would be to make use of the concept of inter-module comparability. If the marking of all of the modules were to be brought into line, then it would be possible to take account of different combinations. Axon (1989) has raised the issue of whether students taking modular courses might undergo a process of academic maturation as they adjust to advanced level ways of working and are able to bring greater numbers of skills and growing competencies to later end-of-module assessments. The number of students involved in the Ridgeway scheme is small so any maturation effects are unlikely to be detectable unless they are very large indeed. Nevertheless, to have raised the issue is important.

The boards will also need to accumulate 'case law' as the system has to respond to all of the special circumstances that will surround the students: the module assessments missed through illness; the students who change their minds over the examination or combination of modules they are working towards; the students who wish to resit a module; the appropriate award to be made to a student who has sat more than the required number of modules; etc.

Quite obviously these issues could not have been explored unless the SEAC had allowed the scheme to be extended to involve other schools and colleges. This permits the comparison of grades awarded through the Ridgeway syllabuses with those awarded for other subjects using traditional schemes of assessment and ones taken by the same students at the same time. The limited expansion of the scheme to some 250 to 300 students is probably sufficient for all of these issues to be explored fully but is still low enough that, in the eventuality of the proposed scheme of awarding encountering problems, the individual students could be put through an award process similar to the boards' normal borderlining procedure.

Some practical problems for A and AS level examiners

The initial AS proposals misunderstood the relationship between depth and breadth in important ways. The debate about AS level standards has therefore had to focus upon two related questions: 'Is it reasonable to expect A and AS level students to perform equally on common elements (questions, sections and papers)?' 'If it is unreasonable, should there be some compensation for the AS level students?'

If the answer to the first question is no and the second yes, this would in practice, almost certainly mean lower paper grade points for some AS level examination candidates. Such a lowering of demand, the DES and SEAC reason, would devalue the AS level examination in the eyes of users. Conversely it can be reasoned that to fail to make such compensation may be to put the AS level students at a disadvantage thereby lowering the popularity of AS level courses and inhibiting the broadening of the sixth form curriculum that underlies this initiative.

It seems to have been assumed that depth and breadth are largely independent so that it is possible to teach depth via reduced breadth. The assumption also seems to have been made that the first is to be valued over the second. The first is questionable. Depth and breadth may not be independent but related in many subtle, and only partly understood, ways. What many people could probably agree about is some of the factors that might contribute to standards. The SEC Annual Report for 1986/7 offered the following examples: the breadth of study; the depth of understanding required; the nature of skills to be tested; the ways that the answers are to be marked; and the ways in which marks are converted into grades. The SEC was in effect admitting the qualitative, rather than the absolute, nature of syllabus demands.

Depth of response may in many subjects be evidenced by the width of experiences that a candidate can bring to bear in answer to a particular question i.e. depth through breadth. The results of the A level grade descriptions exercise would seem to support such an idea. Two of the most highly valued skills demonstrated by candidates in A level examinations are evaluation and synthesis. Both require the candidates to study widely over syllabus material. Therefore, depth of performance in these two skills, and probably other skills, would seem to be dependent upon width of experience.

In many subjects, depth is believed by some educationalists to be related to acknowledged *hierarchies*, although others dispute the idea. Mathematics, the physical sciences and languages are the most commonly quoted examples of hierarchies. Equality of depth would necessitate building the concepts, ideas and skills that underpin these hierarchies in new ways. This is not impossible, but little understood at the present.

Lastly there is the paradox of transfer of learning between subjects, and parts of subjects. One of the principles of AS levels – indeed of broadening the curriculum as a whole – is that a wider range of subjects will result in a larger repertoire of skills that can be transferred to new situations in higher education, in employment and in life. The paradox is that the concept of equal depth used in the initial AS level proposals denies the possibility of transfer between AS and non-AS level parts of the same A level syllabus!

The introduction of the AS level examination has necessitated the extension of the four traditional comparabilities outlined by a fifth and new form i.e. 'the comparability of A and AS level syllabuses in the same subject'. The success of the examination rests on: the willingness of schools and colleges to provide courses; the willingness of students to study AS level syllabuses (whether in complementary or contrasting combinations); and the willingness of the universities and employers to accept AS level results. All three depend upon how this fifth form of comparability is interpreted.

The limited experience already to hand from multi-level subjects (e.g. A level mathematics and A level further mathematics, or physics plus chemistry taken as two subjects when compared with the single subject A level physical science) or instances where examination components were common to more than one syllabus, all seem to indicate that this is unlikely. The possibility that A and AS level students will perform equally on such common elements of an examination is not being dismissed, it is merely being indicated that there are considerable dangers in assuming that they will.

The definitive study on the use of common elements was conducted by Newbould and Massey (1979). They explored the comparability of pairs of A level and pairs of O level syllabuses which shared common elements. They concluded that common components could not be used for equating comparabilities even in the same subject, at the same level. The idea seems, therefore, to have little to offer between levels.

Particularly in subjects such as languages, it would seem inevitable that longer or broader study will result in greater skills and increased knowledge. It is not generally practical to sub-divide – and build a fence around the sections of – A level syllabuses and examinations into those areas of content, skills, and vocabulary which are common to A and AS level and those which are exclusive to A level alone. Similar arguments may (or may not) apply in other subject areas. The problem has best been illustrated by a classicist who upon hearing of the initial AS level proposals commented 'There's no problem. In our A level Latin syllabus there are two passages of translation from Latin to English; in an AS level we need only have one.' The irony of this remark is still lost on many!

In September 1988 the SEC was replaced by the SEAC and so the later stage of the implementation of AS level had to be co-ordinated by this new body. SEAC resolved the issue for 1989 in the first instance by deciding on a rule of no compensation. Qualitative methods could have offered an alternative to the strict application of numerical rules. Indeed the former offer the only approach to A/AS level comparability when the two sets of syllabuses are free-standing and do not share common elements. Whatever the relationships between A and AS level syllabuses, the AS level grades could still be awarded as though the syllabuses were free-standing. The basis for the award of grades could be the Chief Examiners' views of what it is reasonable to expect of examination candidates assuming that they are 18+, have studied the syllabus for the required amount of time spread over two years, and are taking other advanced level syllabuses. It would seem that free-standing AS level syllabuses may well offer the best way forward, unless a complete restructuring of the advanced level system can be undertaken. Free-standing AS level syllabuses have the better chances of coherence and fairness.

This issue will be revisited many times over the next few years.

AS level: some conclusions

It seems likely that the introduction of AS levels will produce a broadening of the sixth form curriculum but not a significant one. AS levels are one approach to the problem and are based simply on the concept of enabling students to study more subjects. A significant broadening of the overall sixth form curriculum will not result unless students come to study four or more AS levels, and this is unlikely. For the individual students, more subjects may not result in broadened personal curricula unless greater encouragement is given to the use of contrasting subjects. Their use is being advocated but they may represent a more difficult option and may, therefore, deter the weaker candidates.

There are problems with AS levels syllabuses as presently constituted. They were introduced at a time when the boards were concentrating on GCSE developments and may not in all cases have been of the highest quality. Suggestions about common components, the use of A level common cores as a basis of AS level syllabuses, confusions over the standards of the new examination and the concept of co-teaching have all proved to be unhelpful.

AS levels are an attempt at an academic solution to a problem that may be wider. Their addition to a student's course, while a step in the right direction, is not a guarantee of the intellectual flexibility that seems to be desired. This would seem to require a more radical solution than was probably acceptable at the time.

There are some basic confusions over AS level standards. Their 17+ origins, and their replacement of AO levels may have misled some teachers about the demands of the new examination. AS levels will be far more difficult than AOs and may be so high as to deter many of the students who took the discontinued examination. While the concept of the parity of esteem between $2 \times AS$ and $1 \times A$ is helpful, the DES and SEAC both seem to have been convinced by their own rhetoric about common components, common marks and common grades. This flies in the face of common and technical sense. Students performances in components of examination are not independent: there is undoubtedly a transfer of skills, knowledge and understanding, not only between components of the same examination but between subjects as a whole. Therefore, those who have studied more of a subject seem likely to do better on the common components. To impose SEAC's current rules for the award of common components may well be to disadvantage AS level students. For the short term the AS level syllabuses without common A/AS level elements seem to be the best way forward but they may be more difficult to resource at the school level.

Despite all of these reservations, the AS level examination is the only attempt to broaden the sixth form curriculum that has so far been introduced – a success but only a partial one. This thinking about standards, in the original concept of the AS level examination needs to be corrected. Further, new links between both of the 18+ examinations and the GCSE must be investigated. If radical changes are to be made in the short term this may well mean that much of the investment in syllabus and examination made by the GCE boards have been wasted. The most important question for further advanced level reform may be: who is to pay for the next round of development?

SIX

The continuing reform of advanced level

The introduction of the first AS level courses, rather than being the start of an interregnum on further proposals for advanced level reform, saw a relative quickening of the pace. The first major initiative was the establishment of the Higginson Committee in March 1987. The Committee's report (DES, 1988c) published in June, proposed new structural changes – this time a system of five 'leaner and tougher' A levels. In common with all earlier proposals for radical structural change they were swiftly rejected.

The setting up of the Higginson Committee and the press discussion of its work had cast some doubts on the future of AS levels and this may have inhibited their early take-up. This uncertainty was confirmed to some extent when the Higginson Report was published and only token endorsement was given to the concept of AS levels. In its rejection of the report, however, the Government reiterated its endorsement of the new 18+ examination.

The second major development was the establishment, under the 1988 Education Reform Act, of the School Examinations and Assessment Council (SEAC) which began work in shadow form in July 1988. This new body immediately began a consultation exercise centred on the issues raised by the Higginson Report. As the 1988/89 academic year progressed and the first AS level examinations approached, the SEAC commissioned and undertook a number of studies into the candidature, subject combinations and, eventually, the results of the first examinations. SEAC also collated some of the experiences of the examinations boards, the schools, higher education and other interested bodies – UCCA, SCUE, etc. From all of this work has come further proposals for change. From the experience of the first AS level awards, and continuing experience with the GCSE, has come a growing realisation that further changes to the 18+ curriculum are inevitable.

Concurrently with the start of the teaching of the first AS level courses in September 1987, that the Government announced the establishment of a Task Group on Assessment and Testing (TGAT) under the chairmanship of Professor Paul Black from Kings College, University of London. The group was charged with advising the Secretary of State on the structure of a National Curriculum for England and Wales and for a system of national assessment. The recommendations of the TGAT Report are outlined in Chapter 4. It is sufficient to say here that although the development of a National Curriculum and National Curriculum assessment is not likely to have effects upon the advanced level system until the early to mid-1990s, the eventual implications of these developments will be significant.

The Higginson Report

The terms of reference of the Higginson Committee were:

> In the light of the Government's commitment to retain General Certificate of Education (GCE) Advanced level examinations as an essential means for setting standards of excellence, and with the aim of maintaining or improving the present character and rigorous standards of these examinations:

> To recommend the principles which should govern GCE A level syllabuses and their assessment, so that consistency in the essential content and the assessment of subjects is secured;
> To set out a plan of action for the subsequent detailed professional work required to give effect to these recommendations.
> (Appendix 1, Higginson Report, DES, 1988c)

In comparison with previous committees that had considered the advanced level examination and its predecessors, this committee was surprisingly small. It was made up of just five people: Dr G.R. Higginson, Vice Chancellor of the University of Southampton; a journalist and broadcaster, a former Chief Education Officer/Vice Chairman of the Secondary Examinations Council; a headteacher; and a manager of Barclays Bank plc. There was also a secretariat of three, including one HMI. In accordance with the usual practice the committee received evidence from a very large number of individuals and organisations, with an interest in the A level examination.

To many concerned with the sixth form, the reasons for the establishment of the committee were unclear. The schools and examination boards were fully committed to the implementation of the GCSE and the AS level examinations. To impose further short term changes on them would have been to risk 'innovation overload'. The most likely reason for the creation of the Higginson Committee was that, having introduced a large number of changes into 16+ examinations, which had achieved a measure of innovation and standardisation to the

115

examination system, the Government wished to introduce similar changes at 18+. By March of 1987 it may also have been possible that the Government had realised that GCSE courses were not, as had initially been hoped, going to be 'end on' to A level and that some short or long term changes would be necessary in order to re-establish the link. Finally, it is possible that having spent so much of their efforts on developing a new system of examination at 16+, the Government had turned its attention to the 18+ examination in – an attempt to redirect attention to 18+ examinations an area of greater interest to their traditional supporters.

The terms of reference contained clear hints that the A level system was to be preserved and that the focus of improvements was to be developments in their quality. The fact that the terms of reference failed to mention AS level was taken by many as a hint that the new 18+ examination was not fully endorsed by the Government and/or higher education establishment. In some press reports early in 1988, however, Dr Higginson was reported as saying that the committee was thinking of proposing the abandonment of the three A level structure in favour of a larger number of subjects. These reports subsequently proved to be accurate. Meanwhile numerous rumours circulated to the effect that the committee's thinking was not finding favour with the Government.

When the report was published in June 1988 the main recommendation of the report – or at least part of it that attracted most attention – was that a five subject structure, using 'leaner and tougher' A levels should be developed. Perhaps the most dramatic part of the whole story was the speed with which the Department of Education and Science rejected the main proposals in the report. In a Parliamentary answer upon the day of publication, the then Secretary of State for Education and Science thanked the committee for the considerable time and energies that they had devoted to the report's production. While their recommendation with respect to the development of the general principles for the A level examinations were welcomed, the committee's main recommendations were rejected for two reasons. Firstly, the Government saw the development of the AS level examination as the key to achieving greater breadth. Secondly, the Government stated its intention to concentrate on the task of introducing the assessment and testing arrangements for the National Curriculum, commenting that the educational service already had a substantial agenda for reform. The responsibility for further 18+ developments was placed in the hands of the School Examinations and Assessment Council.

While the Higginson Committee's proposals for structural reform were rejected, the report also contained numerous suggestions for improving the quality of the A level examination. The report represents one of the few major attempts to harness and accelerate the forces of evolutionary change. For this and other reasons, it is worth considering it in some detail.

Many previous educational reports have been noted for their very careful analysis of contemporary situations, together with the factors and movements that had led up to the establishment of the committee whose findings and recommendations they contained. Given the ways in which the English system of school examinations had been founded, explanations of how an examination came to take its current form must be deemed essential for any complete understanding of the present situation, and possibilities for the future. In short, it is necessary for any report to establish its views on the origins of the system before it is possible to develop, with any validity, the direction in which they then believed the system should go. This the Higginson Report lamentably did not do and many of the failings of the document can be traced to this omission.

In its *one and a half page* analysis of the A level situation in 1988, the report noted that:

- A level was derived from the Higher School Certificate;
- A level is a single subject examination and that this contrasts with the multi-subject nature of continental and American examinations;
- there were eight GCE boards (in England and Wales);
- that the syllabuses were scrutinized by the SEC.

The implications of these remarks were not developed but nevertheless the reader was left with the feeling that the A level examination was deficient as a consequence.

The report noted that A levels were widely regarded as standards of academic excellence, that the best syllabuses offered intellectual challenge by confronting able students with the central concerns of a discipline in stipulating and demanding ways. Good A levels, the report continued, encouraged critical attitudes, thus the development of analytical and interpretative skills. There were also some fundamental problems with the system. Failure to identify with sufficient clarity, the aims, the objectives, the criteria for assessment, were all cited, as was a common perception that over the years syllabuses had become too large. (It was unclear whether this last remark related to the syllabuses as courses of study or as documents.) As a result candidates were overburdened and required to memorise large quantities of information, to the detriment of other and more important aspects of attainment. A levels were also criticised as being too narrow and for encouraging premature specialisation. It was noted that the number of students taking cross-curricular combinations of subjects was increasing, and this was being fostered by the introduction of the AS level examination. The general inability of the A level examination system to respond to change was criticised.

Under the heading 'general principles' the report provided a one sided picture of existing A level examinations mentioning such features as: qualities of mind; rigour; motivation; breadth; balance; depth; relevance; flexibility; practicability; and, cost effectiveness. The implication throughout was that A levels failed to meet these descriptors. The report did not mention the improvements that have taken place in the A level examination over time.*

Having developed a framework of general principles, the report went on to apply these to the examination. It was concluded that the A level examination was too narrow – that three subjects were insufficient. Secondly, it was reasoned that the syllabuses were inadequate in many ways. Token reference was made to the dual system of A and AS level examinations but the latter were generally neglected thereafter.

The main thrust of the report, as indicated above, was that 18+ students should take a larger number – five was suggested – of 'leaner and tougher' A levels. The assumption was clearly stated that it would be possible to reduce the subject content of A level examinations without lowering their intellectual demands. Three very cogent reasons were advanced for this increase in number – broader courses, later career choices, and greater relevance to the world of work and for life. The report did not consider how these new A levels might in practice differ from the AS level examinations then being introduced, nor were any technical implications of the recommendations considered.

In a discussion of the target population of the examination in Chapter 4 of the report, the original candidature of the examination and recent changes in the proportions of 16 to 18 year old pupils staying on were noted. The proportion was, however, judged to be inadequate. Three forms of action to rectify the committee's perceptions of the situation were proposed: further increases in the sixth form population; reduced wastage through more relevant syllabuses; and, making A levels more attractive to potential students. Once again, by implication, the attempt was being made to resolve a problem of society as a whole by modifications to the system of examination.

A large number of objectives for the design of future A level syllabuses were proposed including the very important principles of coherence, effectiveness (not defined), and public accountability. Thinner syllabuses with reduced content would, it was suggested, lead to 'the best teaching methods, courses brought to light, and more highly motivated students'. A number of technical developments in

---

* My greatest personal criticism of the Higginson Report is that on reading it I did not recognise, from the analysis, the system in which I worked. A stereotype of the examination was produced and then criticised.

A level syllabuses were proposed such as the introduction of common cores (although no mention was made of the fact that these had already been developed in 11 A level subjects); general and subject specific principles and assessment criteria, policed by the SEC. (The latter idea was obviously drawn from the GCSE examination.) New contrasting and complementary AS level examinations were also proposed as were modular syllabuses (although it was unclear whether assessment at the end of the course or at the end of each module was being suggested).

Under the heading 'assessment' a number of further principles were outlined (once again despite the fact that some were already to be found in A level syllabuses):

- the extension of existing moves towards the use of oral examinations, extended essays and personal research;

- greater uniformity of boards' practices – awarding procedures, reviews of scripts, borderlines and appeals procedures. Criteria for A level syllabuses was seen as a step towards this aim;

- assessment (grade) criteria;

- in course (teacher) assessment;

- institutional/departmental accreditation (although this idea was not clearly developed);

- differentiation (unfortunately, it was discrimination that was described);

- descriptive assessment;

- profile reporting – neither of the last two ideas were developed.

Under the heading 'organisation' some basic contradictions were evidenced as the report recommended: greater supervision by the SEC; fewer boards; new programmes of research and development; fewer syllabuses; greater understanding of the A level system; greater openness; more informative grades and certificates; improved initial and in-service teacher training; and, somewhat in contradiction, lower examination costs! This part of the report more than any other suffered from a lack of understanding of the features of the GCE system. While making proposals for many improvements in the quality of the examination, the Higginson Committee still required the costs to be reduced. They had even proposed the abolition of some of the boards without considering that it was the competition between them that had kept examination costs at their current low level.

Although the Higginson Report had clearly identified the genuine problems with the A level examination and had made some workable recommendations for change, the report must be judged to be poor. The proposals for structural change of the A level examination were no more successful than any other proposals which would have required alterations to A level standards. Some worthwhile recommendations for improving the quality of the examination were made but existing developments were unacknowledged and inherent contradictions in the proposals not identified. The Higginson Report might have been better received had the committee shown greater understanding of, and sensitivity to, the issues surrounding the advanced level system.

Responses to Higginson

Despite the failings of the Higginson Report, the Government maintained its momentum towards advanced level reform. In September 1988 the Secretary of State for Education and Science asked the newly established SEAC to work towards a rationalisation of the range of A and AS level syllabuses on offer. SEAC was also to reflect on the implications of the Government's response to the Higginson Report and, by the end of June 1989, to offer advice on measures designed to promote the AS level examination and to ensure the appropriate range of good quality A and AS level syllabuses. A SEAC consultation document was published at the end of January 1989 (SEAC, 1989a). Over 3,712 questionnaire documents were issued to schools (both maintained and independent) teaching to 18+, sixth form colleges, tertiary colleges, institutions of further and higher education. A further 312 were issued to educational organisations. About 20% of the former and 50% of the latter responded.

The report, containing the analysis of the responses, indicated clear support for the concept of breadth and the contribution that it could make to the education of individual students. Increased breadth was generally equated with intellectual flexibility, and greater adaptability in higher education and employment. It was also seen as an essential requirement in coping with change – especially technological change – and its implications. Other arguments in favour of either the introduction of greater breadth or other improvements to the GCE A and AS level system were:

(a) *Continuity and progression.* It was pointed out by many respondents to the consultation exercise that the GCE A and AS level system is but one step on the ladder which now reaches potentially from the National Curriculum levels 1 to 10, to the GCSE and onwards beyond the GCE advanced level examinations into higher and professional education. It was also noted that 16 to

19 vocational education courses provide an alternative to the GCE A and AS level system, for many students.

(b) *Strength and weaknesses of existing GCE 18+ examinations.* The now traditional criticisms of the A/AS level examination system were made but on the credit side the examination was still considered to be of value and only a minority of respondents to the consultation exercise seemed to have indicated that they would favour the system being scrapped or radically restructured.

(c) *Compatibility with other European education systems.* It was noted that in other European countries students tend to study far more subjects to 18 and that a very much higher proportion stay on to that point. Once again this point was not discussed in terms of differences of the education system, differences in our structure of examination and different processes of entry to university. Nevertheless, greater compatibility appeared to be an implied future aim. The important point was made that greater breadth of study might prove more motivating to many students and this might indeed encourage greater staying-on.

(d) *Demographic decline.* The point was also made that the proportion of young people in the population will decline and that this could have quite serious implications for the future prosperity of the country, particularly if insufficient numbers of them go into scientific and technological careers. Quoting employers' federations, it was mentioned that employers seldom have to criticise young people for their lack of specialist knowledge rather for their lack of basic skills such as literacy, numeracy, communication skills, analytical powers, social awareness. (The absence of modern languages in this list is of interest.)

Considerable attention was devoted to the concept of a rounded education. Traditionally this has been conceived in terms of bridges across the arts/science divide. The Committee of Vice Chancellors and Principals were reported as having suggested that there were perhaps two routes to a rounded education; through the acquisition of central (common core) skills, or through a wider range of subjects. Schools and colleges that responded drew attention to the significance that they attached to the non-examined curriculum and the provision of broadening experiences – these were commonly considered to include literary and aesthetic appreciation, a study of modern world problems, economic, social and environmental awareness, enterprise ability, citizenship, personal and moral development, and work experience. Here and elsewhere in the report there was an implied discussion of whether these qualities are caught or taught, and therefore whether provision could (or indeed should) be made for them within the examination system.

While most respondents seem to have seen breadth as important, there were few suggestions that it should be achieved at the expense of depth and the positive qualities commonly associated with the GCE examination system. The problem in the achievement of breadth – whether through AS levels or by other means – was seen as being the communication of the concept to students. This in turn depended upon the status that was accorded to a broad education. Nevertheless, greater intellectual breadth was clearly seen to be in the long term interests of the students.

AS level syllabuses as a means of extending breadth

The consultation exercise raised many issues which were, by implication or otherwise, cirticisms of the way in which AS level syllabuses had been developed and introduced. There was evidence of a need for greater independence for the AS level examination. The syllabuses devised by cutting down existing A level syllabuses were not considered to be popular or coherent. No mention was made, however, of problems associated with common A and AS level examination components and questions. This may well be because the consultation exercise took place before the first AS level awards and before the full implications of the SEAC decision on common components, common standards and common grades had been realised.

There was strong support for the concept of the contrasting A level. Indeed, some respondents saw complementary AS levels as even potentially dangerous. The complementary role was, it was suggested, best fulfilled by other A levels. There was much concern over the provision of AS level courses and their teaching. The concept of co-teaching was not popular, although it was acknowledged that this may not necessarily imply common A/AS level content. The possibility of other relationships between A and AS levels that might lead to co-teaching was suggested but not developed. Generally, there was seen to be a conflict between co-teaching and AS level syllabus coherence.

The respondents to the questionnaire seemed to be unclear about the range of AS level syllabuses that should be produced. The report claimed that there was evidence to suggest that proliferation was seen as a danger but it was also indicated that there were issues of A and AS level status. To restrict AS level choices to certain subject areas might be to engender the concept that A level was the more difficult, and therefore had the higher status.

'Support for AS courses in broader-based subjects, perhaps covering fields of learning or experience, was strong among approximately two-thirds of schools and colleges. Arguments put forward in favour of such courses included:

(i) the relative ease with which breadth of experience may be planned and implemented through such courses;

(ii) the relative ease with which non-specialist needs could be met;

(iii) the creation of opportunities for introducing 'new' subjects not tied too closely to established disciplines;

(iv) an improved structure for co-ordinating the development of core skills and facilitating the transferability of those skills;

(v) a greater chance of providing subjects that bridge the arts–science divide;

(vi) a greater chance of bridging the academic–vocational divide and of establishing linkages with vocational education organisations;

(vii) avoidance of a situation where students may "pick and mix" courses without reference to any guiding concept or structure;

(viii) an improved framework for fostering the study of crosscurricular themes that help to place subject-specific learning within a wider context of, for example, social, economic, political and environmental understanding;

(ix) the provision of an avenue for studying the applied aspects of subjects and the implications for society as a whole;

(x) improved opportunities for progression from certain pre-16 initiatives, e.g. TVEI programmes.'
(p. 28, Section 4, Document 2, SEAC, 1990a)

The issue here is quite clearly one of coherence in individual students' study programmes.

The development of these broader-based courses would require, as the report suggested, the establishment of guiding criteria. These would be necessary, it was reasoned, to avoid the trivialisation of AS levels, lead to the development of broader based courses, while at the same time not permitting their proliferation. It was acknowledged, however, that clear signals of acceptability of broader-based courses would be required by higher education and employers before they would become popular. The links between such courses and existing general studies provision were not made.

A second area of possible development was that of skill-based courses. When the views of the responding educational organisations were collated the following suggestions appeared:

- modern foreign languages, for scientists and engineers
- information technology/computing
- statistics

- mathematics with an emphasis on applications/numeracy
- use of English

The issue must be raised of exactly how many courses of this sort a student could take while still achieving the specialisation that seems to be desired for the more able. The hope was expressed that through the use of the broader-based and skill-based AS levels, the system could prove of value to many of the students who currently do not take A or AS levels.

Advanced level examinations

The consultation exercise revealed overwhelming support for the retention of A levels. On the positive side they were seen as engendering qualities such as rigour, challenge, and stimulation. Students who had successfully taken A levels were considered to be good at conceptualisation, to have good analytical skills, the ability to think, and the ability to assimilate knowledge. A levels were seen as standards of excellence, as a route to scholarship (a concept that had not been referred to for some years) and as probably the best assessment of existing and potential capabilities. It was proposed that the quality of A levels could be improved by the use of more investigative work plus more varied, and appropriate, forms of assessment.

A levels were also seen as having many unfortunate negative qualities including:

 (i) narrow academic orientation with a restricted knowledge base;

 (ii) over-burdened content, sometimes unrelated to the real world, which restricts conceptual understanding and application, too great an emphasis on memory and recall;

(iii) an inadequate range of assessment methods with possible implications for teaching and student progress;

(iv) inadequate attention given to the relationships between different areas of study, resulting in a narrow perspective;

 (v) insufficient opportunities for students to take a measure of responsibility for their own learning, to explore issues and to solve problems;

(vi) narrow knowledge base possibly poor predictive ability, inadequate as preparation for employment;

(vii) the principle of differentiation is not being applied, its achievements are not formally acknowledged unless they successfully

124

complete the whole course and examination, there is a lack of short term goals to maintain motivation.*

Further criticisms made were the lack of clear links with further education courses for students aged 16 to 19 (viii), the multiplicity of different syllabuses and the implication of this for higher education (ix), and occasional variation in the difficulty of different subjects (x).

It was unclear from the report whether these criticisms were general or applied to particular subjects, syllabuses, and/or boards. The criticisms were fair to an extent. Some are less true now than they used to be (i, ii, iii, ix). Some are traditional problems of subject-based examination systems (iv, v). Some criticisms are probably applicable to particular groups of students only (vi). It is the less able that tend to enter employment directly from their advanced level courses. At least two of the criticisms are the result of the 'goal posts having been moved after the ball was kicked' (vii, viii). The remainder are current Government 'hobby horses' (viii, ix, x).

It is very difficult for any system to defend itself against generalised criticisms of this sort. Examples can always be found to illustrate (in the eyes of those complaining at least) the points being made. The SEAC analysis is unhelpful as it stands but did lead to action. If all of these criticisms were generally true then the advanced level system should be scrapped forthwith. On SEAC's own admission the A level system has many strengths. Nevertheless, the need for reform is clear, especially in certain respects if not the whole.

Criticisms, which until recently might have been levelled at any section of the British education and examination system, were also focused on the A level examination. Chief among these was the observation that students that fail in the A level system take nothing with them except their sense of failure. The lack of continuity between GCSE courses and A and AS level examinations was also mentioned but as suggested elsewhere, the fault for this does not lie with the A level system, which has done much in the short term to try to bridge this gap.

This SEAC consultation exercise is important in three ways:

(a) It tried in its latter stages (paragraphs 45 to 47) to tackle the issue of curricular breadth. Although it was only a little more successful than previous attempts, it did make the interesting point that there are three essential elements to a learning experience – factual content, skill development and styles of assessment. These combined together, it was proposed, offered a total experience that needed to be appropriately balanced.

---

* With one exception the principle of differentiation (the production of different courses and examinations for students of differing ability) has not been applied at A level. One SMP mathematics syllabus has been developed with a limited grade range.

(b) The report established a framework for the way ahead which will be considered in more detail in the next chapter. A major plank of this work was that SEAC wished to exercise control over the system through a set of guiding principles or criteria. Paragraphs 55 to 57 of the SEAC report proposed a very large number of developments, many of which were derived from the Higginson Report.

(c) Most significantly, the report began to see parallels between the GCE A/AS level system and other courses for students aged 16 to 19 offered through colleges of further education and examined by organisations such as City and Guilds of London Institute (CGLI) the Business and Technician Education Council (BTEC) and the Royal Society of Arts (RSA). The value of the vocational aspects of sixth form education were stressed to a far greater extent than previously; in later reports and discussion papers the possibilities of common stepping stones and the transfer of credit were both developed.

The SEAC Consultation report (SEAC, 1989a) must be criticised on one important count, namely, it did not consider any of the technical issues surrounding syllabus development or examination construction. Fortunately, this was recognised in later papers. The eventual report *Advanced and Advanced Supplementary Examinations* (SEAC, 1989b), containing the advice of the Council was forwarded to the Secretary of State for Education and Science in mid-July of that year.

The SEAC also prepared a detailed analysis of existing advanced level provision. The further report thus set its discussions on a very much firmer basis having conducted a major consultation exercise during February to April 1989, rather than relying on evidence submitted. It was noted that 434 A level syllabuses were on offer in 1988 and that this number declined by 10% to 390 for 1990. 170 AS level syllabuses were on offer in the same year – obviously the processes of syllabus proliferation was already well established at AS level. While the consultation showed that support for a broader curriculum from 16 was virtually universal, many of its findings with respect to the AS level examination were far from encouraging. Firstly, there was considerable confusion about the standards of the examination. For example, the relationships between depth and breadth of study and between the demands of A and AS level examinations were not understood by users. (This was not surprising.) Secondly, the AS level examination is not compulsory and, therefore, its value has to be demonstrated. Partly as a result of both of these issues, the AS level examination was considered to have 'less currency' than A levels. Some teachers, and subsequently their students, believe that the AS level examination represented a standard midway between GCSE and A level. While many schools and colleges required AS level syllabuses that were co-teachable with their A level equivalent, there was some widespread disaffection with those syllabuses that had been derived by a vertical division of an A level syllabus. These were generally seen as lacking in coherence and integrity. Nevertheless, the report suggested that if all involved with the examination played their part, the problems could be resolved.

There were two further areas of concern identified in the report. Students were tending to favour complementary AS level subject combinations, and so the examination was not achieving the degree of broadening of students sixth form courses that had been hoped for. The instance of cross-curricular subject choices, particularly those that might bridge the art/science divide, were rare. Further it was considered that far too many schools were using AS levels as steps towards A level examinations rather than as courses in their own right.

In a joint survey with the NEEDS project (SEAC, 1989a) it appeared that few AS level entries were the result of a genuine attempt at a broader curriculum: over 50% of the hundred centres that had replied by mid-June 1989 expected students to go on to A level in the same subject in which they had entered for AS.

The SEAC report concluded that the provision of AS level courses would be assisted by greater clarity in their principal role and an emphasis on contrasting studies. The report went on to propose steps that it hoped would improve the acceptability, the technical efficiency, and the overall broadening of the sixth form curriculum that might result from further AS level developments. These suggestions were embedded within proposals for a gradual restructuring of the advanced level curriculum as a whole and at both A and AS levels. Further, the quality of syllabuses would be aided by the introduction of general principles to govern A and AS level examinations. New arrangements for the development and approval of revised syllabuses were suggested based on a test of need. Some experimentation was to be permitted – the Ridgeway scheme was offered as an example – and the SEAC A and AS level scrutinies were to continue.

In its analysis of the existing advanced level system, the SEAC report acknowledged that AS level development was not proceeding in the direction that the Government desired. The report recommended that sixth formers would need to achieve a balance between the depth of specialist study and the breadth in the number of subjects studied. This could be achieved, it was reasoned, without detriment to the rigour and intellectual standards associated with the A level examination.

The problems of encouraging AS level development were acknowledged and a continuing multi-focus approach was advocated. It was

127

recognised that the AS level examination is not compulsory and that students willingness to study it was dependent on many factors including the number of courses on offer and their perceived currency for admission to higher education and to employment. A major problem surrounding the examination was acknowledged to be misunderstandings about its status with respect to the A level examination. The SEAC report reiterated the previous policies by stating: that the AS level required the same intellectual rigour as the study of A level but required only half the teaching and study time; that AS levels were not intermediate in standard between the GCSE and the A level examinations; and, that A and AS level syllabuses represented mutually supportive aspects (it is not possible to use the term 'complementary' in this context) of advanced level achievement.

The SEAC report broke with previous traditions and began to discuss the skills which might be engendered by the study of A and AS level examinations in terms of the perceived needs of the individual and of society as a whole. Emphasis was placed upon the continuing development of skills especially in the communication and numeracy areas. In short a small, but significant, step was being made in proposing an overall rather than a piecemeal policy for 18+ examination development. Links between the A and AS level examinations and other 18+ examinations, indeed other examinations in general, were made through discussion of the role of the NCVQ. (National Council for Vocational Qualifications).

Looking to the future the SEAC report concluded that there might be three ways in which AS level courses could be developed:

(a) AS level courses in single subjects (the present model);

(b) AS level courses in broad-based subject areas, e.g. science, social science;

(c) skill-based courses in areas such as information technology, modern foreign languages and vocationally orientated areas more commonly covered by the examinations of CGLI, BTEC, and the RSA.

The second of these recommendations is something of a surprise. In the development of GCSE examinations such hybrid areas of study have not tended to receive favour from the present Government. The report also broke new ground by looking forward to the development of abilities within other areas, possibly within non-examination provision, for example social, economic and political awareness, and artistic appreciation. In proposing these developments a wider view of the role of 18+ examinations in the education of the student as a whole was being proposed.

In some ways the SEAC was also setting the clock back towards more traditional views of sixth form courses, the ways in which such

128

courses should be developed, and the ways in which they should be assessed. The discussion of features of the AS level examination and its relations to A level aside, few of the proposals were new. Many had occurred several times throughout the history of the development of the Higher School Certificate and the A level examination. What was unusual in terms of recent reports was their combination and positive discussion within a single document.

The other facets of the SEAC report concentrated on a very much tighter and centralised control of the examination system. These proposals included the development of general principles for A and AS level syllabuses, these might relate to subject areas rather than to single subjects as have been the case in the GCSE National Criteria. These would include:

(a) rules for the rationalisation and approval of syllabuses;

(b) greater parity of standards between different syllabuses;

(c) clearer guidelines for the development of A and AS level sylla- buses and ensuring the intended relationship between them;

(d) the establishment of appropriate balance between knowledge, understanding and skills in both A and AS level syllabuses;

(e) the establishment of clear links between 18+ examinations, 16+ examinations and Key Stage 4 of the National Curriculum.

Without specifically mentioning it, the SEAC proposals would do much to develop an examination and assessment system incorporat- ing both breadth and depth. A and AS levels were recognised as a step on the ladder linking the National Curriculum Key Stages 1 to 4, plus the GCSE, to higher education and employment. Similarly, links sideways from the GCSE, via 16 to 18+ vocationally orientated courses of the RSA, CGLI and BTEC were proposed. These vocational courses would provide alternative routes into both higher and extended professional education.

A programme of development was proposed and the report con- cluded by suggesting that 1994 provided an appropriate target date for the improved and strengthened advanced level examination (incorporating both A and AS level developments) to be fully in place.

Current developments

The way forward for the A and AS level system was pointed by Clive Hart, the recently appointed Assistant Secretary of the SEAC with responsibility for the 16 to 18+ curriculum. His paper *AS Exam- inations: The Future* (Hart, 1989) was presented at a one-day DES conference held in November 1989. He announced the establishment of four working parties, charged with formulating new principles for the advanced level system. The paper outlined developments since the production of the Higginson Report and reported on the consultation exercise (SEAC, 1989a). Hart noted that in September 1994 the first pupils who will have experienced Key Stages 3 and 4 of the National Curriculum will enter post compulsory education in order to embark on advanced level work. SEAC was anxious to ensure adequate progression from the National Curriculum and to provide opportunities for increasing numbers of 16 to 19 year olds – whether they proceeded through the GCE advanced level system or through more vocationally orientated routes. The aim was to 'extend their learning and understanding in directions relevant to their individual needs and the needs of society'.

Hart went on to consider what and who AS level examinations and courses were for. He reiterated the official line concerning the target population, the purposes of AS levels, their content, and coverage with respect to A level. The paper contains some softening of the SEAC thinking on the standards of A and AS level examinations suggesting that the idea of equality of standard was not an easy concept to grasp. He also suggested, drawing on ideas from the National Curriculum, that it would be helpful to think of there being fewer attainment targets for AS than for A level courses. Nevertheless, the levels of performance to be expected within these attainment targets would be common to both. Using this new line of reasoning it was, nevertheless, pointed out that AS levels were intended to be two year courses and that it is expected that the students taking them would be taking other GCE advanced level courses.

In an oblique reference to the decision of the SEAC earlier that year to impose the concept of common components, common marks and common grades, it was also noted that a smaller proportion of candidates achieved grades A to E through AS levels than at A level. Drawing on provisional figures released by the GCE boards, he noted that 61% of AS level students gained grade A to E as opposed to 76% at A level. Perhaps in an attempt to explain this difference he then went on to report that approximately 62% of the candidates who had entered for the new examination were aged 17 or less. This points to some AS levels being studied over one year rather than two. (Whether this accounts for all of the difference, or whether it was also partly due to aspects of current policies on awards is not yet clear.) Hart notes that many of these grades are probably considerably lower than the students might have expected to achieve. This may also be due to remaining confusions with the standards of AO level examinations. From these data it would seem that many students are using the AS level examination as a stepping-stone to A level and not necessarily as a means of broadening their programmes of study (once again shades of Q and F). It is also important to note that the two most popular AS level subjects within the sample were mathematics (14,000 entries out of a total of just under 35,000) and general studies, (8,700), both previously 17+ (AO) courses. Hart argues that there is only one level – the advanced level standard, but there are two examinations – the AS and A. However, for consistency with earlier chapters the terms A level and AS level will continue to be used here.

From Hart's discussion of the breadth of the curriculum we see for the first time, in a semi-official document, an attempt to go beyond a mere listing of desirable qualities that might follow from such a process and vague links to desirable outcomes of the personal, economic and social nature. Hart recognises that while much is claimed for the benefits of breadth, and there are many ways to its achievement, it has tended to remain a difficult concept to unpack and to realise through examination syllabuses.

From the SEAC's consultation exercise (SEAC, 1989a) six contributory sources of breadth are discerned:

- experience of a wide range of subjects;
- aquaintance with the links between subjects;
- development of important general skills and competencies;
- contact with different modes of learning;
- experience of using skills to apply knowledge;
- contact with the consequences of using knowledge.

Given adequate development of these suggestions and their appropriate implementation in syllabuses, it seems likely that their achievement would indeed go a substantial way to producing the mental flexibility so long desired.

In what amounts to a further dimension of the concept of broadening, Hart revived aspects of the two cultures concept of Snow given in his Reith Lecture of 1959 (see Allanson et al., 1967) including: the importance of bridging the arts/science divide by fostering both literacy and oracy in potential scientists, and providing arts students with continuing mathematical studies. This was advocated as one means of providing experience of a wide range of subjects. Although Hart is quick to point out that breadth is not confined to the building of relatively simple bridges between clusters of disciplines. What is required, he suggests, is exposure to a broader range of the concepts, skills, and ideas which underpin individual disciplines. It does not necessarily have to be achieved, of course by the study of more subjects. It can be fostered, he reasoned, by the establishment of links between subjects and by helping students to develop understanding of concepts drawn from scientific, technological, human, social, and economic domains. Breadth, he suggests, should not be divorced from mainstream experience and then bolted on as a semi-discrete

131

extra, rather it should be derived from a commonly planned and co-ordinated series of experiences.

While conceding that it is quite unrealistic to expect any one type of examination course to assess achievement across all six of the above elements in a balanced way. The SEAC consultation report suggests that the best syllabuses should encourage critical attitudes, develop analytical skills and involve students in a wide range of activities involving oral, written and practical work, very often of an investigational nature. To some extent this flies in the face of two important factors. Firstly, A level examinations are already compli-cated. Even the new AS level examinations which were introduced for first examination in 1989, have tended to be more complex, often several times more complex, than the first A level examinations of the early 1950s. To propose, in effect, further forms of assessment might well indeed be to overload the assessment system to breaking point. If these new and balanced assessments were not applied care-fully and rigorously there would be a serious risk that assessment would actually encroach further into the processes of teaching at sixth form level. Secondly, to demand that all syllabuses offer the very qualities that Hart has listed, to some extent conflicts with the subject nature of the examination. Not all subjects lead naturally to the study of all of the desirable areas of experience. Nevertheless, the identification of the skills and experiences inherent in different subjects, and possible subsequent addition to them, does offer a model for use in the planning of individual student's courses. The problem is, can they all be included without risk of student overload and/or some diminution of the traditional concepts of rigour?

The paper does not appear to depart from the previous thinking on the numbers of A and AS level subjects to be studied by individual students. Hart sees advantages inherent in, say, two AS plus two A levels, over a pattern of provision based on 'examination courses of a homogeneous nature' (A levels alone). This does not necessarily constitute a major broadening of a student's curriculum, unless as Hart has suggested elsewhere in his paper, the AS levels are used for contrasting purposes. The general take-up of five or six A levels by individual students, was not discussed but would appear unlikely for some years to come.

He also offered reassurances on the issues of choice by stating that the SEAC did not see its role as one of restricting the development of subjects, rather of preventing the proliferation of syllabuses. Access to minority subjects is to be preserved.

Hart expanded on the concept of broad-based subjects at advanced level suggesting that:

- 'the relative ease with which breadth of experience may be planned and implemented through them;

- the creation of opportunities for introducing "new" subjects not tied too closely to established disciplines;
- a greater chance of providing courses which bridge the arts/science divide;
- improved framework for fostering and study of cross-curricular themes which might help to teach subject specific learning within a wider context, for example, social, economic, political and environmental understanding;
- the provision of an avenue for studying the applied aspects of subjects and the implications for society as a whole;
- a greater chance of bridging the academic/vocational divide.'

(paragraph 22, Hart, 1989)

These may require, of course, the development of new, and additional, methods of assessment. These would have to be cross-curricular in nature, as to do otherwise would be to sub-ordinate their study to the traditional subject approach. It would not, after all, be possible, when teaching a cross-curricular theme to make assumptions about the skills being developed in the other subjects that students might be studying.

Hart also touched on the concept of parity between the academic and vocational qualifications post-16. The foundations of this discussion had been laid in SEAC (1989a) but was further developed by Hart. In a discussion of his paper which appeared in *The Times Educational Supplement* on 1 December 1989, it was reported that agreement had been reached by the Employment Secretary (then Norman Fowler) and the Education Secretary (Mr MacGregor) on a joint system. The National Curriculum Council (see NCC, 1990) had been working with the National Council for Vocational Qualifications to identify five levels of progressive attainment related to approximate academic equivalence: shown in Table 4.

Table 4 *Proposed links between the GCE and vocational systems*

level	example of vocational qualification	academic qualification
1	basic test of practical competence at work	old CSE examination
2	more advanced competence test such as City and Guilds CGLI 7061 or BTEC first	5 GCSEs
3	BTEC national diploma	A level
4	technician or management diploma (higher national diploma)	diploma in higher education
5	professional institute examination	university degree

(TES, 1 December 1989)

In conclusion Hart identified a list of areas on which further action or movement was needed:

- the continuing development of advanced level teaching;
- the issue of A/AS level comparability and the establishment of a single advanced level standard;
- the use of contrasting and complementary combinations of subjects;
- the take-up of AS level.

The SEAC working parties

The membership of the four SEAC working parties was announced towards the end of 1989. Each was charged with a particular aspect of formulating the general principles for advanced and advanced supplementary examinations.

They were all given both general and specific tasks, and in addition all working parties were required to:

(i) to develop general principles in order to provide controls on standards, syllabus development, syllabus quality and progression from GCSE;

(ii) to formulate these general principles in sufficient detail in order that they may be used as instruments to direct the process of syllabus construction, syllabus approval, and the assessment of candidate performance and the conduct of examinations;

(iii) to liaise with the other working parties as appropriate and, where necessary take into account their recommendations;

(iv) to prepare a report specifying (i) and (ii) and, in some form, detailing the working parties' main deliberations and decisions.
(p. 76, SEAC, 1989a)

Working party A: syllabus structure and development

Working Party A had a very detailed brief which covered all aspects of syllabus development including relationships with other examinations, new developments, the developing National Curriculum, and the European dimension. All this was in addition to any of the factors which had already become accepted parts of GCE examination syllabuses. In short their brief was:

> to formulate the principle governing components and structure of A and AS examination syllabuses in the interest of consistency between syllabuses in the same and different subjects.

The committee was chaired by Professor R. Pring of the Department of Educational Studies, University of Oxford. It consisted of nine people drawn from higher education, schools and examination bodies. In common with the other three working parties, there were also assessors from Her Majesty's Inspectorate, the National Curriculum Council and the Curriculum Council for Wales.

Working party B: A–AS inter-relationships

Although the terms of reference of this working party were briefer, and reiterated many of the features which had underpinned the development of the AS level examination, working party B probably faced the most difficult and far-reaching task. In short they were asked:

> to formulate principles governing the nature of and inter-relationships between A and AS syllabuses with due regard for (a) both depth and breadth of study, (b) the common advanced level standard shared by both examinations and (c) the establishment of a suitable range of both examinations in schools and colleges.

Working party B was chaired by Mrs C. Bowering, Head Teacher, Nottingham High School for Girls. The committee consisted once again of nine members. There were both people from higher education and from schools, plus one person could be said to have had substantial experience in the administrative, curricular and technical issues surrounding 18+ examinations. This person was the late Mr R. Blackburn, Deputy Director General, from the London Office of the International Baccalaureate. Given the topics to be considered, this committee contained few people with a technical background in assessment.

Working party C: assessment and reporting

The detailed terms of reference of this working party incorporated both principles that had clearly been drawn from the National Criteria for GCSE and from later thinking on 18+ examinations. In short their terms of reference were:

> to formulate principles (a) governing approaches to, and patterns of, assessment for both A and AS examination courses and (b) relating to the reporting of individual achievement and results.

The working party was chaired by Mrs P. Perry, Director, South Bank Polytechnic. The membership of this committee was made up of three representatives of higher education, one school teacher and a number of people drawn from examination bodies.

Working party D: conduct of examinations

This working party had perhaps the least exciting task. Detailed terms of reference were supplied reflecting many of the more important features of the more recent evolution of both GCE advanced level examinations and school examinations in general. Despite these remarks the importance of the work of this committee cannot be underestimated. Working Party D, perhaps more than the others, was charged to lay the ground rules for future A and AS level syllabuses and the technical and administrative procedures which must underpin the result and examinations. In addition they were asked to give attention to the in-service training for teachers (INSET). In brief they were required:

> to formulate principles governing the conduct of A and AS level examinations in order to ensure that their operation is commensurate with (a) the establishment of an improved and strengthened advanced level examining system and (b) the principles recommended by Working Parties A, B and C.

The committee was chaired by Professor D. Lawton, University of London School Examinations Board and Chairman of the Consortium for Assessment and Testing in Schools (one of the agencies that had been charged with the development of National Curriculum Assessment materials for Key Stages 1 and 3). The membership of the committee was drawn exclusively from examination boards and groups (one member represented the Joint Council for GCSE, the remainder the GCE system).

The National Curriculum Council and core skills 16 to 19

As the work of the four SEAC Working Parties was drawing to a close, the National Curriculum Council in March 1990 issued a response to the Secretary of State's remit of November 1989 (see National Curriculum Council, 1990). Building on ideas drawn both from the National Curriculum and other work in the 16 to 19 age range – both academic and vocational – the NCC proposed a framework for the whole curriculum 16 to 19 which included themes, guidance and core skills.

Five cross-curricular themes from the 16 to 19 curriculum were identified:

- economic and industrial understanding;
- environmental education;
- education for citizenship;

- careers education and guidance;
- health education.

It was suggested that these themes were also essential in the post-16 curriculum and that up to 16 the main emphasis had been on:

- social and economics and understanding

For work in typical A and AS level programmes of study these themes were extended to include:

- scientific and technological understanding;
- aesthetic and creative understanding.

In developing briefly the concept of guidance, reference was made to student choices, programmes of study, review procedures and preparation for further stages in a student's career. The value of records of achievement regular assessment and reviews of progress were stated.

In the discussion of core skills the NCC, drawing upon the work of other bodies, identified six core skills which it believed should be incorporated into programmes of studies for *all* 16 to 19 year olds:

- communication;
- problems-solving;
- personal skills;
- numeracy;
- information technology;
- modern language competence.

The models proposed were complex. The NCC suggested that the six core skills should be embedded in A and AS level syllabus wherever possible, be a requirement of syllabus design, and should overlap and reinforce one another but remain identifiable. It was suggested that records of achievement could be used to indicate students' progress through the matrix of 18+ subjects and the core skills that they might contain.

In the assessment of core skills and subjects the National Curriculum Council proposed a system based upon the National Curriculum Key Stages 1 to 4. This was to involve use of:

- attainment targets;
- programmes of study;
- assessment arrangements.

For example it was suggested that an attainment target should be clearly defined, with levels of attainment, each of these six core skills.

A fundamental part of the NCC proposals was the concept of credit accumulation and transfer between academic and vocational courses. The ideas discussed by Hart (1989) were developed and a structure involving 'units of competence' and 'elements of competence' was proposed. The first were to be sub-divisions of a qualification and the unit of accumulation. The second were to comprise the units of assessment, the equivalent of the National Curriculum Statements of Attainment.

The NCC model in the core skills 16 to 19 is a complex one. It has to be contrasted with the generally more practical model inherent in the terms of reference of the SEAC's working parties. Firstly, the NCC model may prove extremely complex to implement in syllabus terms. Secondly, it might well prove difficult, even unwieldy, when applied to the recording of an individual student's progress through the matrix of core skills and subjects. Thirdly, the relationship between the matrix and cross-curricular themes was not fully developed. The latter issue is important given the likelihood that the curriculum 16 to 19 would remain subject-based. While it seemed likely that those responsible for syllabus development, teaching and the examination of A and AS level courses would be able to exploit the cross-curricular links, it is unlikely that they would be prepared to sub-ordinate their specialisms to what might be somewhat ill-defined cross-curricular themes.

Concurrent developments

In parallel with the NCC and SEAC endeavours in the 16 to 19 curriculum, work continued apace on the implementation of the National Curriculum 5 to 16. From September 1989 and increasingly as the months of 1990 passed, it became clear that the National Curriculum might prove to make unreasonable demands upon teachers. The teaching of the National Curriculum and the recording of attainment targets covered was proving difficult. The assessments – teachers' assessments and standard assessment tasks – were being trialled at Key Stage 3 and piloted at Key Stage 1, and were proving even more difficult to implement. As the pilot study of Key Stage 1 assessments proceeded, manageability for teachers became an increasingly important issue. Partly because of demands on the National Curriculum, partly because of the introduction of local management of schools and partly for other reasons, teacher morale declined. In London in particular, the abolition of the Inner London Education Authority and the reorganisation of education under the Inner London Boroughs, caused further difficulties. By the time therefore, that the SEAC working parties reported and their deliberations were collated, anything which would have made excessive demands upon teachers – either in the presentation or assessment of their courses – had become unthinkable. What then, did the four SEAC working parties propose?

The way ahead – some thoughts

One of the fundamental problems of reforming the advanced level curriculum is that it is sandwiched between new developments within the National Curriculum and GCSE, on one hand, and a fairly solid refusal by higher education to contemplate major changes, on the other hand. If the National Curriculum, possibly in combination with the GCSE, is successful then it is likely that more – and younger – students will enter into what has traditionally been the sixth form. These students will create new demands on the system. If the structure of the advanced level system – its syllabuses and its organisation – are reformed along the lines indicated, then this will to a certain extent take some pressures off the post-18 curriculum in further and higher education. If the SEAC reforms now beginning produce more efficient courses and therefore some diminution in the demands on post-16 courses, why should the 16 to 18 system itself not share some of the resulting benefits? If universities and polytechnics no longer have to deal with the diversity of courses, and therefore have to spend (waste) less of their time on orientating former A level students to degree courses, might this not be grounds for some small diminution in agreed standards of the advanced level examinations? This would permit more time to be spent on the broadening effects that everybody seems so much to desire.

SEVEN

A view of A and AS level examinations in the mid-1990s

Background

The SEAC working parties A to D completed their tasks in April 1990. Their recommendations were compiled and reconciled in a report entitled *Draft Principles for Advanced Supplementary and Advanced examinations* (SEAC, 1990b) which was submitted to the Council's 18+ Examinations Committee in May. The report as a whole was discussed by the members of the four Working Parties in June and was approved for distribution to outside bodies by the Council in July. A public consultation followed during September to October, and the final report will be available early in 1991.

Like all who have attempted to reform the advanced level system, the SEAC Working Parties, and the staff responsible for collating their ideas into an overall report, faced major difficulties. Firstly, comparisons with the Higginson Report, were inevitable. Further, they faced the same fundamental problems of all who have attempted to reform the advanced level system, namely, of how to broaden the curriculum and widen access to the examination without reduction in its intellectual standards.

The report was presented in the form of 33 draft principles for AS and A level syllabuses and examinations. The structure of the report was as follows:

an introduction;
a preamble;
Section I, Principles for Syllabuses;
Section II, Principles for Assessment and Reporting;
Section III, Principles and Procedures for the Conduct of AS and A examinations;
a glossary of terms;
two addenda.

The tone of the report, particularly the principles for syllabuses, was traditional, stressing the need to maintain academic standards. However, embedded within the principles are radical ideas for broadening the advanced level curriculum, for widening access, and for new approaches to assessment. Approval of the document, or even some of its main ideas, will lead to a new era of advanced level developments, and will culminate in the introduction of new syllabuses in 1994. This is a short time scale. Much work will have to be undertaken by the GCE boards and SEAC working together, before the revision of syllabuses can begin.

The report begins with a short rationale, which sets out the main aims of the principles:

- to 'play a full part, together with the National Curriculum in securing an overall improvement in the country's educational standards;

- to ensure 'contemporary suitability of AS and A examinations' so that examination courses will be able to 'play a positive and effective role in contributing to a broader curriculum post-16 . . .' and provide 'a clearer and better system of opportunity for all students in the post-compulsory phase of education';

- to serve as 'guarantors of syllabus and examination quality', by providing 'a necessary framework for syllabus develoment and approval'. (Introduction, paragraphs 1–3).

The report reveals some of the tensions encountered by the working parties:

- how to avoid the proliferation of AS and A level syllabuses, while still maintaining choice and quality;

- how to promote AS level examinations, while maintaining a single advanced level standard.

In advice to the Secretaries of State, SEAC recommended that the development of syllabus guidelines will enable SEAC to:

- exercise control over standards at advanced level;
- guide the construction of AS and A level syllabuses;
- improve the parity of standards between different syllabuses;
- provide a means of implementing the intended relationship between AS and A level examinations;
- balance the knowledge, understanding and skills in both levels of syllabuses;
- provide the most appropriate forms of assessment;
- provide continuity and progression from the GCSE and Key Stage 4 of the National Curriculum.

141

The role of the GCE boards in bringing about these changes and the need not to escalate costs are both acknowledged.

Section I – Principles for syllabuses

Principle 1 ranges over the desirable qualities of AS and A level examinations. It is suggested that all advanced level syllabuses should ensure adequate breadth, balance, rigour and depth. Further, the traditional subject base of the syllabuses is stressed:

> AS and A level examinations must be founded on a selected body of subject specific knowledge (content), skills (including [core skills]* and a scheme of assessment which together promote the study of specific disciplines and their associated techniques and methods of investigation. (Principle 1b)

> Depth and rigour involve the initiation of students into the common concepts and language which underpin disciplines. Students learn to recognise both explicitly and implicitly what constitutes grounds for arguments and the test for truth within disciplines. They also acquire awareness of the methodology of disciplines, including what constitutes evidence, and the procedures that may be used to expose new evidence, to develop new lines of argument and to criticise existing arguments and evidence. Depth and rigour arise from the learning opportunities that allow students to gain experiences of disciplines by active involvement in their essential processes, for example, through problem solving and active enquiry. Ultimately, students should be in a position to appraise critically the received notions and methodology of the disciplines that they have studied. However, skills and concepts should be developed in such a way that, potentially, they may be applied to unfamiliar context. (Principle 1f)

These two comments constitute the clearest endorsement of the value of subject based study since the Crowther report.

Principle 1 also stresses the need for:

- clearer learning goals;
- progression from Key Stage 4/GCSE studies;
- continuity with higher education, further training and employment;
- the need for breadth of learning and experience through the incorporation of core skills and cross-curricular themes into advanced level examinations;
- the encouragement of attitudes of curiosity and enquiry;
- the consideration of the linguistic and cultural diversity in society;
- the avoidance of biases;
- improved administrative procedures.

---

* The SEAC report places square brackets around the term [core skills] to indicate the provisional nature of the idea.

Finally, it is suggested that in appropriate subjects there should be links with courses leading to vocational qualifications.

Principle 2 reiterates the now familiar statements that AS and A level examinations should be of the same standard, should both require two year courses, but necessitate different teaching and study times. It is suggested that AS level syllabuses should be designed to represent 120 to 135 hours of teaching time, and A levels twice this amount.

Principle 3 is revolutionary. In muted language, it suggests that the basic unit of advanced level courses should become the AS level, rather than the A level as at present. It is concluded that 'the AS examination course should embody the essential skills, knowledge and learning that constitute the advanced level standard'. The A level course should provide 'the additional contexts in which students can develop further and illustrate their grasp of the discipline.'

The Committee proposes that the normal full-time advanced level programme should be made up of the equivalent of six AS level units, rather than three A levels as at present, with each student taking a recommended minimum of two AS level examinations. For this to be workable, it is suggested that AS level courses would need to be available in a wide range of subjects and subject areas. The working parties considered that the terms 'complementary' and 'contrasting' should not be attached to the name of individual syllabuses.

In the name of syllabus uniformity, Principle 4 proposes the establishment of subject cores, to replace the existing A level common cores. These subject cores are to be developed in at least the National Curriculum core and foundation subjects, and those with GCSE National Criteria. This suggested list is not exhaustive. Principle 5 begins the process of standardising syllabuses by setting down the criteria for the use of subject titles.

Principle 6 extends the concept of modules. It sees them, in effect, as mini-syllabuses, each requiring 40 to 45 hours of teaching time. It is proposed that modules should be assessed partly during the course and partly at the end. It is also suggested that all advanced level modular syllabuses should conform to a common set of patterns. It is not a requirement that modules should be taught consecutively.

It is also proposed that some flexibility should be permitted in the way individual modules are used in courses and qualifications. An important distinction is made between an 'inwardly modular' structure and an 'outwardly modular' one. The first is seen simply as a device for structuring syllabuses, or for offering schools and/or students an element of choice, perhaps on a core and option basis. The second permits the modules of one subject to be used in different combinations with those of other subjects. The report suggests that clear rules will be necessary in order to ensure coherence of study.

Students may also be given up to five years to complete the pattern of modules for any one advanced level subject.

The standardisation process continues with Principle 7 which establishes a provisional set of rules for syllabus structure. The rules range in nature from the purely administrative – e.g. 'the syllabus must give the date of first approval by SEAC' – to major intersubject initiatives. The remaining ideas are a mixture of:

- new SEAC thinking on the central control of the examination system;
- updated ideas about syllabuses derived from the GCSE National Criteria, the National Curriculum, and the current advanced level system;
- new ways of encouraging breadth of study.

Like Principle 1, Principle 7 contains some radical, but muted, proposals for the redesign of the advanced level system. The idea of cross-curricular themes is developed. They are to link one subject with another, and show relevance to working life. The awareness and understanding of economic, political, social, aesthetic, cultural, health, environmental, and technological factors relevant to the subject, including the European dimension, are to be encouraged.

All syllabuses may also have to contain a clear statement of the core skills that they contain and assess. Any further development of the concept will be dependent upon the Secretaries of States' response to the idea. The examples of core skills given are: applications of numeracy; applications of technology; scientific and technical awareness; economical awareness; aesthetic appreciation and modern foreign language competence.

One of the administrative innovations of Principle 7 is that the syllabus for any one subject must include everything that a student or teacher will need to know, including the set books and instructions for the marking of centre-assessed components.

Section II – Principles for assessment and reporting

Principle 8 contains, what may be seen by traditionalists as, further radical proposals for the assessment of advanced level syllabuses. Once again the ideas are derived from a variety of sources. For example, the use of a variety of assessment techniques – hitherto a characteristic of English school examinations in general – is now to be a requirement. Further, the concept of positive achievement, developed in the GCSE, is now to be applied to the advanced level system. In addition, three new ideas are proposed: firstly, the transfer of credit between the GCE and other systems of qualifications; secondly, the introduction of records of achievement; and thirdly the increased use of criterion-referenced assessment. Elsewhere in the report, the possible use of Statements of Attainment* and systems of levels are proposed for the assessment of the core skills.

The need to avoid excessive demands upon students, in respect of both the content of syllabuses and their assessment, is acknowledged. It is suggested that A level syllabuses might use a wider variety of assessment techniques than the AS level. While the value of projects and individual studies at A level is endorsed, it is suggested that these should not be compulsory at AS level.

Principle 9 concerns the desirable technical features of assessment. Once again very little of the content of this principle is new to English assessments and examinations. It is the way in which existing features are bought together which is original. Principle 10 considers the potential role of formative assessments in AS and A level examinations. It begins by stating unequivocally that the overall scheme of assessment for full-time students must combine coursework assessments with a final examination (the terminal assessment). It is recommended, however, that the overall assessment scheme should include no more than 40 per cent coursework. The distinction is made between *board-assessed* and *centre-assessed* coursework components, and it is suggested that some syllabuses may come to use combinations of both.

Future AS and A level examinations should be capable of contributing to a record of achievement that would note down progress, knowledge, understanding and skills attained during a period of study. The record should provide recognition of work completed and skills achieved by students, even if they do not complete their advanced level course. This record should also serve to foster links with the vocational and other systems of qualifications. It has yet to be decided whether these records of achievement will be board and/or otherwise certified.

The idea of a record of achievement fits well with SEAC's proposals for the development of modular courses. The end-of-module results, whether school or board assessed, are to form part of the final results. In addition, a final inter-module, end-of-course examination will also be required comprising 25 to 40 per cent of the total marks. The record of achievement may also become the mechanism for the banking of end-of-module assessments.

Principle 11 again stresses the need to maintain advanced level standards. All formal assessments are to contribute directly to the final grade awarded. There are to be no hurdles or grade enhancement schemes, using optional components. As part of a major innovation, *all syllabuses* are to contain grade descriptions for the award of grades A, B and E. This is to extend existing work of the GCE

---

* Statements of Attainment are the basic units of National Curriculum assessment. See the TGAT Report (DES, 1988c).

boards. Principle 12 reiterates the value of assessing students in positive terms. It goes on to recommend the award of a *profile* of results rather than a single subject grade as at present. It is also proposed that success in any component which contributes at least 20 per cent to the final marks be included. Lastly, SEAC expresses the intention to explore ways of reporting a wider range of attainment, including positive achievement which falls below the existing grade E level. Although no new system of grades is proposed, the implication is obvious. If a new system of advanced level grades were to be introduced it would offer an opportunity to remove the anomaly in the grading of the GCE and GCSE systems.

Principle 13 concludes the section on assessment and reporting by requiring standardised methods and by stressing the needs of students, parents, employers, and further/higher education.

Principles and procedures for the conduct of AS and A level examinations

This third and longest section of the report contains 20 principles, very many of which are either restatements or extensions of existing features and trends. Only those which are new, or suggest significant developments, will be discussed in detail.

Principle 14 makes an unequivocal statement that the conduct of AS and A level examinations should be fair to candidates; and that fairness appears to be equated with consistency. In a major departure from current and past thinking, the report proposes that the fairness of the system would be enhanced if representatives from schools, higher education, further education and, wherever possible, industry and/or commerce, play a part in setting the advanced level questions. In the past this has been exclusively the domain of chief examiners appointed for the purpose. Teachers, whether in schools, colleges or in higher education, often do play a part in question or paper moderation. Other professionals also have a role in vocational examinations but not at advanced level.

Principles 16 to 20 concern administrative matters including: the provision of materials for practical components; the need for candidates to understand precisely what it is that they are required to do; the responsibilities of chief examiners for their components of the examination; and the conduct of the coordination meetings at which the marking scheme is explained to all assistant examiners. These reflect current good practice, with the additional emphasis that demands made upon students and schools must be reasonable.

Principle 21 is likely to prove extremely difficult and expensive to implement fully. It requires that comparable standards should be applied to the marking of centre-assessed and board-assessed components. While stating that the teachers should be fully briefed, and that appropriate assessment criteria and/or mark schemes should be consistently applied, mechanisms for the development and use of these criteria are not discussed. Presumably, these are to be left to the boards to devise.

Carrying on the theme of the reasonableness of demands upon students and schools, Principle 21 also requires that all written coursework assessments – whether individual studies or projects – which generate at least 15 per cent of the final examination marks, should require prior approval by the GCE board. The purpose of this proposal is to ensure the appropriateness of the proposed work. Current board practice on this issue varies.

Principle 22 raises the issue of coursework moderation, i.e. the need to ensure that the assessments received from different schools and colleges are comparable. It does not discuss how comparability is to be achieved or how the necessary resources and inherent costs are to be found. Somewhat surprisingly, the principle contains an apparent endorsement of statistical moderation.

Principles 21 and 22 extrapolate developments which began with the large scale introduction of coursework as part of the Certificate of Secondary Education (CSE). As described in Chapter 1, two approaches to the achievement of inter-school comparability have been used by the boards. The first is pre-assessment standardisation, using mark criteria, detailed instructions, samples of work etc. The second is post-assessment moderation using samples and/or statistical techniques. While it is possible to achieve a substantial measure of comparability using basic techniques, it has been acknowledged for some time that the achievement of complete comparability may be impossible and would require the expenditures of greater quantities of time and money than current resources permit. Principle 22 fails to consider either how the issue of comparability is to be approached, or what degree of success is to be achieved. These issues need to be resolved if the use of coursework components is to become a less emotive issue.

Principles 22 and 24, respectively, concern the standardisation of the marking of individual assistant examiners, and the grading of AS and A level examinations. In the latter, it is the comparability of standards over time that is emphasised. The many factors which need to be addressed at a crucial phrase of the examination are identified. In general, they are intentional re-statements of current good practice, but there are also some points of particular interest. Firstly, current procedures for the achievement of comparability between AS and A level examinations are to remain. Given the tone of the repeated SEAC pronouncements about the need to maintain standards any other policy would probably be politically unthinkable. Secondly, the importance of grade descriptions and samples of work are stressed as aids to the judgement of the A/B, B/C and E/N grade boundaries.

Paragraphs 25 to 33 lay down guidelines for the various administrative activities which follow the grading of AS and A level examinations, i.e. the reporting of results (25); the provision of feedback to teachers (26); the appeals procedures (28) (the establishment of an independent appeals authority by SEAC in November 1990 is noted); the administrative demands on centres (29); students with disabilities and others in need of special consideration (30); private candidates (31); malpractice and misconduct (32); and common procedures for dealing with borrowed papers (33). The only element of these later principles which departs from existing good practice is number 27 which re-emphasises the responsibilities of the boards in provision of inservice training (INSET) for new examinations.

What do the SEAC guidelines have to offer?

The guidelines produced by SEAC (1990b) must be seen as a significant advance on that produced by Higginson et al. (1988). The former is supported by thorough investigations and preparation. It has also made use of a very large number of informed people, familiar with the organisation and details of GCE examinations. It may be said that the SEAC report has harnessed some of the contemporary evolutionary developments with radical ideas for broadening the curriculum and, in effect, merged them within a single set of proposals.

The principles for syllabuses offer a useful consolidation of the best of the existing AS and A level examination system. By building on existing good practice, the principles have the potential to enhance the high public esteem in which the advanced level system is currently held. Rather than merely setting a requirement, as the Higginson report did, for better syllabuses, the SEAC principles contain ideas for their achievement. There seems every reason to believe, whether the more radical proposals listed in section II below are introduced or not, that the principles will produce a clearer, fairer and thus more efficient advanced level system.

The SEAC principles also contain a radical agenda for reform which includes:

(a) The elevation of the status of AS levels. If AS levels are to be the basic unit of advanced level study, it is the A level examination which will become the supplement. It would seem appropriate, therefore, to rename AS levels. They are in effect, the 'Advanced Standard'. In a curricular sense, however, AS level syllabuses remain supplementary in nature.

(b) AS level syllabuses will also vary in nature. It is recommended that they should be available in single disciplines, combinations of disciplines, and in broad-based subject areas such as science, social sciences and the performing arts (Principle 1c). The last of these will have an inherent broadening effect, but integrated courses of this kind do not always attract high public esteem.

(c) All syllabuses are to show how they encourage and assess a number of important core skills. These have the potential to link subjects to produce more coherent programmes of study.

(d) Inter-subject links are also to be developed via a series of cross-curricular themes.

(e) The links between one subject and another, and the applications of subjects are to be stressed.

(f) Subject cores are to be established for all National Criteria core and foundation subjects, plus subjects for which there are GCSE National Criteria.

(g) There are to be grade descriptions for the A/B, B/C and E/N grade boundaries. It is not completely clear from the report whether the development of these will be undertaken by individual boards, or the boards working collectively with SEAC.

(h) The principles take forward the concept of modules and their assessment.

(i) Records of achievement are to become a feature of advanced level examinations in the same way that they are in the primary and secondary phrases of education.

(j) The current system of single advanced level grades is to be supplemented by a profile. This will list performance in any component which contributes at least 20 per cent of the final subject marks.

(k) As in the case of the GCSE, coursework components are to become a feature of all systems of advanced level assessment.

(l) Systems for transferring credit gained by the study of vocational and other qualifications are to be introduced.

If all of the above proposals – or indeed a majority – are well received and successfully implemented, they will represent a major development in the structure of the examination. It would be necessary, however, to ensure that all of the ideas are capable of working in combination. The proposals (with the possible exception of core skills seem both practical and desirable, given our current state of knowledge and experience. Clearly, there is

149

much preliminary work that will have to be done to create the various structures outlined above, before the work to develop syllabuses can begin.

There were some omissions in the report. It has, for example, little to say about:

- Special papers – the implication would seem to be that they are to be discontinued.
- General studies and its potential contribution to the broadening of sixth form courses.
- The value of specific methods of assessment other than coursework (formative) assessments. However, the use of a variety of assessment techniques is stressed.
- The current number of General Certificate of Education examination boards.
- The need to change the current system of grades. However, the consultation exercise will explore the issue of broadening reporting to reward positive achievement below Grade E.
- The suitability of AS levels as one-year courses.
- The potential costs of the innovations proposed and how they will be funded.

The broadening of sixth form courses

The elevation of the status of AS levels, the variety of forms of AS levels, the assessment of core skills and the introduction of cross-curricular themes, the development of the concept of syllabus modules, and the introduction of records of achievement, will all serve to broaden sixth form courses if they are adopted by all levels of the educational system. In addition, the stressing of links between one subject and another, the introduction of profiles, and the increased use of coursework assessment will all assist to varying extents in this process.

The development of core skills

The concept of core skills embedded within different subjects is interesting, but may be difficult to realise. It is easy to see how the central skills of communication, problem solving, and personal effectiveness could be developed in almost every subject, although the nature of these skills may vary from one subject to another. It is also possible to see how some of the core skills identified – applications of numeracy, applications of technology, scientific and technical awareness, and economic awareness – might be developed in many subjects. Indeed, the process may be well under way.

The concept of core skills, after the change in the status of AS levels, is probably the most radical proposal contained in the SEAC proposals (SEAC, 1990b). Clearly much work will have to be done before they can become a practical feature of future advance level syllabuses. All of this is acknowledged in the report.

The SEAC has already begun work on the development of core skills and it is from this that the ultimate decision on introduction will depend. Even if they are not adopted, the thinking and work behind the concept of core skills will be of value. It is many years since inter-subject issues received such detailed attention at advanced level.

It seems unlikely that every syllabus can be expected to incorporate aspects of all core skills. Similarly, it is unlikely that many students, when selecting their advanced level subjects (be they AS or A levels), would be likely to choose a combination which provides a full coverage of all core skills. To seek to achieve comprehensive coverage of these skills might be to run counter to other aspects of the SEAC proposals.

Many people will feel that subject matters should not be subordinated to inter-subject links. It would be counter productive if the achievement of a suitable advanced level profile required students to achieve successes in too complex a grid. If this were to happen it would be all too easy for critics to suggest that the real aim of the exercise – the broadening of the system – had become subverted into something akin to an intellectual stamp-collecting exercise.

There are several administrative problems that need to be addressed. Who, for example, will assess and record the Statements of Attainment which will make up the core skills? The answer in both cases is, presumably, the teachers. Given that it is likely that many students will take AS and A levels of more than one board, who will be responsible for the accumulation of the inter-board results and their conversion into levels? Will the levels be reported syllabus by syllabus or as part of a single summative assessment? If it is the latter, who will resolve the inevitable problems as some students' attainment in the skills assessed in any one subject vary considerably from the attainments in the same skills in different subjects? The need is for trials to establish basic case law. The potential complexity of some of the accumulating and accumulated patterns of results is illustrated in Figures 3 and 4 respectively.

The results of the consultation exercise may be crucial in the decision that the Secretaries of State will make on the future of core skills.

Improved access to advanced level studies

The main initiatives, to encourage a large number of students to study at advanced level, place requirements on the boards to develop more interesting syllabuses and to ensure that they are accessible to

ANYTOWN SIXTH FORM COLLEGE

Student's name ————————   Date of entry ————————————

Subject —————— Board —————————— Level: AS/A/Other ————————

COURSEWORK AND/OR MODULE ASSESSMENTS

	DETAILS/NO.	CENTRE/BOARD	ASSESSED	MARK/GRADE	MODERATION
i					
ii					
iii					
iv					
v					
vi					
vii					

SPECIAL TOPICS/PROJECTS

TITLE	DATE APPROVED	MARK/GRADE	MODERATION

ASSESSMENT OF CORE SKILLS

| NAME AND REFERENCE | SKILL NO. 1 | SKILL NO. 2 | SKILL NO. 3 | SKILL NO. 4 |

Levels and statements of attainment

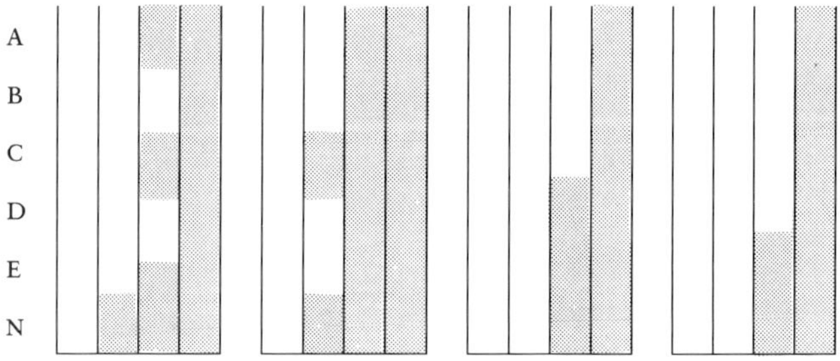

A
B
C
D
E
N

FORMATIVE FEEDBACK AND OTHER NOTES (AND DATES)

(*Note* Records of homework, practical, and other assessments which do not contribute directly to the award of grades are to be kept on the back of this form.)

Figure 3 *A hypothetical advanced level formative record*

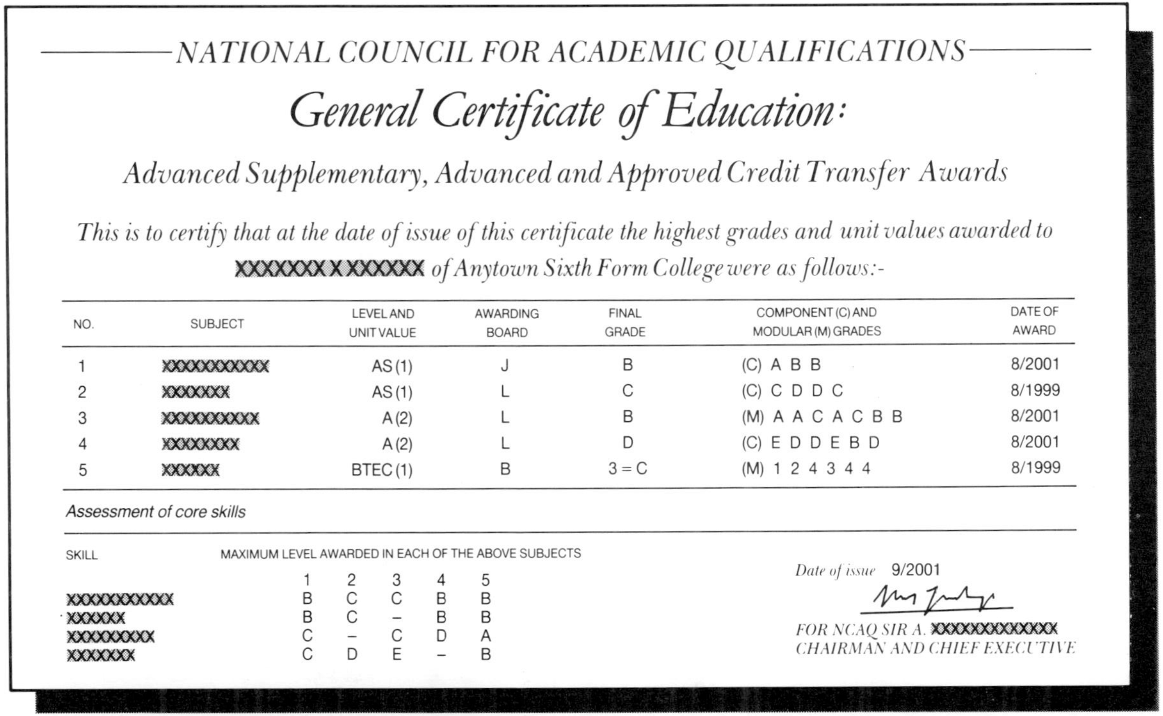

─── NATIONAL COUNCIL FOR ACADEMIC QUALIFICATIONS ───

General Certificate of Education:

Advanced Supplementary, Advanced and Approved Credit Transfer Awards

This is to certify that at the date of issue of this certificate the highest grades and unit values awarded to
XXXXXX X XXXXXX *of Anytown Sixth Form College were as follows:-*

NO.	SUBJECT	LEVEL AND UNIT VALUE	AWARDING BOARD	FINAL GRADE	COMPONENT (C) AND MODULAR (M) GRADES	DATE OF AWARD
1	XXXXXXXXX	AS(1)	J	B	(C) A B B	8/2001
2	XXXXXXX	AS(1)	L	C	(C) C D D C	8/1999
3	XXXXXXXXXX	A(2)	L	B	(M) A A C A C B B	8/2001
4	XXXXXXX	A(2)	L	D	(C) E D D E B D	8/2001
5	XXXXXX	BTEC(1)	B	3 = C	(M) 1 2 4 3 4 4	8/1999

Assessment of core skills

SKILL	MAXIMUM LEVEL AWARDED IN EACH OF THE ABOVE SUBJECTS				
	1	2	3	4	5
XXXXXXXXXX	B	C	C	B	B
XXXXX	B	C	–	B	B
XXXXXXX	C	–	C	D	A
XXXXXXX	C	D	E	–	B

Date of issue 9/2001

FOR NCAQ SIR A. XXXXXXXXXXXX
CHAIRMAN AND CHIEF EXECUTIVE

Figure 4 *An example of the kind of certificate that advanced level students may be receiving by the end of this decade*

students who have obtained at least level 7 of the National Curriculum. In addition, the extension of the concept of modules, the use of records of achievement and, most importantly, the facility to transfer credit gained in the study of vocational qualifications, will all serve to encourage more students to undertake A level courses. The last, in particular, will indicate that the skills students bring from the other systems are both relevant and valued.

The maintenance of standards

Despite the repeated assertions in the report that standards will be maintained, it will be very difficult to demonstrate that the Principles have been successful in doing so. The SEAC report contains few suggestions about how, precisely, such stability will be achieved. It is likely that the evaluation of advanced level standards will move further in the direction of criterion referencing.

Some of the changes recommended by SEAC run counter to current popular prejudices. The proposal for increased coursework have already caused adverse comment by more traditionalist elements of educational and public opinion.*

SEAC appears to have pinned its hopes for maintaining standards on two strategies. The first is the introduction of subject cores, and the second is the development of grade descriptions for the A/B, B/C and E/N grade boundaries. These may well serve to ensure greater comparability over time in future years. The number of changes being proposed by SEAC is so large, however, that the standards of future advanced level examinations will be different from current ones. While the advanced level examinations remain even in part norm-referenced, there will be little bases from which to compare standards across time, especially when the system changes significantly. Unfortunately prejudice tends to rule in such cases, and it is far too easy to see all changes as retrograde.

On the other hand, the proposed relationship for the new AS and A level syllabuses is clearly more practicable than the existing one. To define a new system of AS and A level syllabuses and examinations, with clear relationships between them, is far more likely to achieve comparability than to attempt to 'bolt on' AS levels to an existing A level system which had been designed before AS levels were thought of.

---

* See the articles by John Clare in the *Daily Telegraph*, 5 September 1990, and by Robin Reeve in *The Times*, 11 September 1990.

The consultation exercise

The SEAC report (1990b) was circulated, for information, to all schools and colleges providing post-16 education. It was also issued for discussion to all local education authorities, universities, polytechnics and other institutions of higher education, plus approximately 200 other interested organisations.

Views were sought on each principle in turn, and the exercise focused in particular on:

- AS/A level inter-relationships;
- subject cores, including KS4/GCSE links;
- 'guarantees' about essential features of disciplines;
- the relationship between the subject cores and AS/A level syllabuses. (Comment was invited on whether the AS level syllabus should equate to the core or whether it should be greater than the core);
- the proportion of coursework marks which should be contributed to the award of grades;
- the number of years over which modules should be banked;
- the development of grade descriptions;
- the desirability of extending the grading scale;
- component/holistic grading;
- the usefulness of the glossary.

Comments were not requested specifically on the concepts of core skills and cross-curricular links.

A strong endorsement of all, or a majority of, the proposed developments would strengthen the hand of SEAC when it comes to deal with traditionalist elements within schools (both independent and maintained), the universities, and the DES. A positive response may well determine the degree of radicalness of the revised system.

The implications of the SEAC report

The main issue to be considered here is what the SEAC proposals will do for the student and for society. Will they prove to be more difficult in their demands? Will they generate the greater breadth and wider access that are anticipated in a coherent and straightforward way?

Implications for students

For the more able students, the Working Parties' proposals will produce greater breadth. The proposals offer these students many choices and opportunities to demonstrate achievement. If schools and colleges are able to provide sufficient ranges of courses, the more able student will be freed from the necessity to specialise. Coherence, previously associated with the study of cognate subjects, can now be achieved through the cross-curricular links. With the opportunity to study more subjects to the 'advanced level standard', through the systems of core skills, it is to be hoped that the developments will go a significant way to producing the greater intellectual maturity and flexibility that has so long been demanded of good A level students. With the closer specification of syllabus content and learning outcomes, it seems likely that all of these features can be achieved without diminution in academic rigour.

The proposals also have much to offer the less able student. Through a process of credit accumulation they will be enabled to work at their own pace. Topics which, within the existing GCE system might have proved difficult, can now be reinforced and developed in different ways through the systems of core skills, and cross-curricular links. The concepts of banked modules, and transfer of credit with the vocational systems, should do much to encourage students to enter the more academic branches of post-16 education. More importantly, the proposals should assist these students to achieve, albeit in slightly different ways, and on slightly modified timescales.

It is the middle-ability advanced level student for whom the system has, immediately, slightly less to offer. While these students will be offered more interesting courses, the ranges of choices could prove confusing, even distracting. Unless counselling and academic planning within their institutions is good, they may find themselves striving to make use of all of the opportunities on offer. While the systems proposed are intended to provide flexibility and interest, they could, for many, prove something of an intellectual orienteering course.

Implications for schools

The implications of the Working Parties' proposals for the AS and A level examinations are complex, and will require, as the GCSE and the National Curriculum have already required, greatly improved systems of academic planning and coordination. The staff, in the institutions which teach to advanced level, will need to have a clear understanding of the system and be able to counsel students appropriately. They will also need to develop structures within their schools and colleges to forge and maintain the teaching of the core skills and cross-curricular links. SEAC will be offering further advice on this issue.

More importantly, administrative procedures will need to be put in place to record the students' progress as it takes place. Once again, these needs are not unique but, parallel to those created by Key

Stages 1 to 4 of the National Curriculum. It seems likely that the responsibility for assessing and recording students' achievement against the statements of attainment which make up the [core skills] will also fall upon the schools. Further, merely to record is not sufficient. It is important that the accumulating records are used as a basis for regular discussion with the student about his or her progress. The problem is, can all schools and colleges provide the resources to implement the necessary courses? Will it all take too much teacher time? Timetable exercises and trials are needed soon to confirm the practicability of the proposals.

Implications for examination boards

These will be substantial. The ideas have yet to be sufficiently developed to constitute a blueprint for the production of the new examinations. Further work will be necessary when outline approval is given to individual principles. There is also going to be a period of experimentation as each board produces schemes within the individual subjects for the realisation of all of the ideas proposed. With the huge investments that will be required of the boards to develop the new syllabuses, it may well be that not all syllabuses will be produced by all boards. Indeed, SEAC may 'license' boards to develop syllabuses in some specified subjects. Some boards may not even have the resources to take part in this exercise and may be forced to merge or close.

There will also be a need for a new form of organisation. The examination boards (whether working individually or collectively), SEAC or even the LEAs, will need to collate and certify students' progress through the examination syllabuses of different boards. While individual schools and colleges will be able to record the cross-curricular links, the modular successes, the vocational links, the cross-curricular themes, as they are studied, it seems unlikely that individual institutions will be given responsibility for the inter-subject certification which the SEAC proposals seem to imply. An academic equivalent of the NCVQ will be necessary.

SEAC also proposes a review of the principles after five years and this may well prove necessary. Five years is sufficient time for the ideas to be implemented, initial small problems to be resolved, and longer term evaluations of what is necessary to be produced. For the boards, this means that they must recover the costs of syllabus development in this time. The result of this financial constraint may be reduced choice.

Implications for higher education

The implications for higher education are also significant. On the credit side, advanced level students who have taken the broadened programme should bring to their higher education courses a broader academic preparation. This should, in turn, produce an enhanced intellectual maturity. Despite the increasing complexity of the 18+ examination system, it is to be hoped that it will show more clearly what has been studied and what the grades awarded imply.

On the other hand, it is to be hoped that the specialist faculties in higher education – physical sciences and engineering, and possibly modern languages – will not continue to insist on three A levels, but will be prepared to accept students with a broader base. The whole success of the SEAC's ideas may hinge on the attitudes of these high status subject communities.

One of the possible responses of the more traditional university departments may be a demand for longer degree courses. Perhaps, after all, this is justified? Is it reasonable to expect the sixth form curriculum and the GCE advanced level system to continue to bridge the gap between, on the one hand, the changes created by the National Curriculum and the GCSE, and on the other, changes within higher education? The value of broader higher education courses and the resultant need to extend their duration is already recognised. Pressures on some engineering courses, mainly as a result of the professional requirements of the engineering councils for a broader professional education, have already led several universities to extend the usual three-year degree courses to four years.

The GCE advanced level system in the mid-1990s and beyond

At best the SEAC proposals are a starting point for a new round of structural changes, of syllabus development and of new examinations. Too many of the ideas are untried in practice and implementation of them may itself be a process of adaptation and evolution. It therefore seems that far from coming to the end of the problems of the advanced level examination system, we are only at the stage of having a basis for real reform.

The English system of A/AS level examinations is already distinct from other Western examination systems. Unlike the others it can also be considered as a kit of parts from which shhools, colleges and students can build their own courses. If the new proposals are successfully implemented, then something quite new will have been created. Rather than just being concerned with their own logic and language, subjects will become the means of generating general intellectual skills. These skills will also, hopefully, serve to bond the system together as never before. The SEAC proposals amount to more than a series of changes to the GCE advanced level system, they could well be the foundation of something more akin to an English Baccalaureate.

Bibliography

ALLANSON, J. T., *et al.* (1967) 'Towards a Broader Curriculum,' *Nature*, **215**, 23 September, pp. 1329–34.

AXON, T. M. (1989) 'The Comprehensive Experience' in HUGHES, J. J. (ed.) (1989) *AS Levels: Implications for Schools, Examining Boards and Universities*. London: The Falmer Press.

BARDELL, G. S., FORREST, G. M. and SHOESMITH, D. L. (1978) *Comparability in GCE: A review of the boards' studies 1964–77*. Manchester: Joint Matriculation Board on behalf of the GCE Examining Boards.

BLACKBURN, R. (1988) *A. D. C. Peterson, OBE, D.Ed. (Hon): 1908–1988, a tribute*. Geneva: International Baccalaureate Office.

BLAKE, D. L. (1989) 'The Experience of a Sixth Form College' in HUGHES, J. J. (ed.) (1989) *AS Levels: Implications for Schools, Examining Boards and Universities*. London: The Falmer Press.

BOARD OF EDUCATION (1938) *The Organisation and Curriculum of Sixth Forms in Secondary Education*. London: HMSO.

BRUCE, G. (1969) *Secondary School Examinations: Facts and Commentary*. London: Pergamon Press.

CENTRAL ADVISORY COUNCIL FOR EDUCATION (ENGLAND) (1959) *15 to 18*. The Council (The Crowther Report). London: HMSO.

COHEN, L. and JOHNSON, S. (1982) 'The Generalizability of Cross-Moderation', *British Educational Research Journal*, **8**, 2, pp. 147–58.

COMMITTEE OF VICE-CHANCELLORS AND PRINCIPALS (1970) *The Curriculum and Examinations in the Sixth Form*. London: The Committee.

DEPARTMENT OF EDUCATION AND SCIENCE (1980a) *Proposals for a Certificate of Extended Education* (The Keohane Report). London: HMSO.

DEPARTMENT OF EDUCATION AND SCIENCE (1980b) *Examinations 16–18: A Consultative Paper*. London: HMSO.

DEPARTMENT OF EDUCATION AND SCIENCE (1984) *AS Levels: Proposals by the Secretaries of State for Education and Science and Wales for a Broader Curriculum for 'A' Level Students*. London: HMSO.

DEPARTMENT OF EDUCATION AND SCIENCE (1985) *GCSE National Criteria*. London: HMSO.

DEPARTMENT OF EDUCATION AND SCIENCE (1986a) *Better Schools*, DES/Welsh Office (Cmnd. 9469). London: HMSO.

DEPARTMENT OF EDUCATION AND SCIENCE (1986b) *Broadening Your A Level Studies, Advanced Supplementary (AS) Levels: a guide for Schools and Colleges*. London: HMSO.

DEPARTMENT OF EDUCATION AND SCIENCE (1986c) *Broadening Your A Level Studies, Advanced Supplementary (AS) Levels: a guide for Students and Parents*. London: HMSO

DEPARTMENT OF EDUCATION AND SCIENCE (1987a) *Broadening Your A Level Studies, Advanced Supplementary (AS) Levels: a guide for Schools and Colleges*. London: HMSO.

DEPARTMENT OF EDUCATION AND SCIENCE (1987b) *Examination Reform for Schools*. London: HMSO.

DEPARTMENT OF EDUCATION AND SCIENCE (1987c) *The National Curriculum 5–16: A Consultative Document*. London: HMSO.

DEPARTMENT OF EDUCATION AND SCIENCE (1988a) *A Student's Guide to AS Levels*. London: HMSO.

DEPARTMENT OF EDUCATION AND SCIENCE (1988b) *AS Levels off to a Good Start*. Press Release 36/878, 28 January. London: DES Press Office.

DEPARTMENT OF EDUCATION AND SCIENCE/WELSH OFFICE (1988c) *Advancing A Levels: Report of a Committee appointed by the Secretary of State for Education and Science and the Secretary of State for Wales*, (The Higginson Report). London: HMSO.

DEPARTMENT OF EDUCATION AND SCIENCE (1988d) *Report of the Task Group on Assessment and Testing (TGAT), a Report*. London: HMSO.

DEPARTMENT OF EDUCATION AND SCIENCE (1989a) *Report by HM Inspectors on GCE Advanced Supplementary Examinations: The First Two Years*, The Department, INS56/12/365.

DEPARTMENT OF EDUCATION AND SCIENCE (1989b) *The National Curriculum: From Policy to Practice*. London: HMSO.

ENGINEERING COUNCIL et al. (1988) *AS Levels are Important*. A joint statement by the Council in conjunction with other bodies (including the CVCP, SCUE, and CNAA).

EYSENCK, H. J. (1953) *The Uses and Abuses of Psychology*. London: Pelican Books.

FORREST, G. M. and SHOESMITH, D. L. (1985) *A Second Review of GCE Comparability Studies*. Manchester: Joint Matriculation Board on behalf of the GCE Examining Board.

FORREST, G. M. and VICKERMAN, C. (1982) 'Standards in GCE: Subject Pairs Comparisons 1972–1980', *Occasional Publication 39*. Manchester: Joint Matriculation Board.

GCE BOARDS OF ENGLAND, WALES AND NORTHERN IRELAND (1963) *Common Cores at Advanced Level*, The Boards.

HARRISON, A. (1983) 'Profile Reporting of Examinations Results', *Schools Council Examinations Bulletin No. 43*. London: Methuen Educational.

HART, C. (1989) *AS Examinations: The Future* in the report of a DES Conference of the same name held on 22 November 1989. London: DES.

HARTOG, P. J. and RHODES, E. C. (1936) *The Marks of Examiners*. London: Macmillan.

HEADMASTER'S ASSOCIATION (THE) (1968) *The Sixth Form of the Future.* London: The Association.

HUGHES, J. J. (ed.) (1989) *AS Levels: Implications for Schools, Examining Boards and Universities.* London: The Falmer Press.

INTERNATIONAL BACCALAUREATE OFFICE (1985) *General Guide,* 5th ed. London and Geneva: IBO.

INTERNATIONAL BACCALAUREATE ORGANISATION (1989) *The International Baccalaureate: An Organisation, International Curriculum and University Entrance Examination.* London and Geneva: IBO.

JACKSON, R. (1989) 'Government Policy on A and AS Levels', in HUGHES, J. J. (ed.) (1989) *AS Levels: Implications for Schools, Examining Boards and Universities.* London: The Falmer Press.

JOHNSON, S. and COHEN, L. (1983) *Investigating Grade Comparability through Cross Moderation. Programme 5 – Improving the Examinations System.* London: Schools Council.

JOINT COUNCIL FOR THE GCSE (1987) *Modular GCSE Schemes: Their Development and Assessment,* Working Paper No. 1. Manchester: JMB for the Council.

JOSEPH, SIR K. (1984) 'Speech to the North of England Education Conference, Sheffield, January', in SECONDARY EXAMINATIONS COUNCIL (1985) *Report of the Draft Grade Criteria Working Party: English.* London: The Council.

KING, A. R. and BROWNELL, J. A. (1966) *The Curriculum and the Disciplines of Knowledge: A Theory of Curriculum Practice.* New York: Wiley.

KINGDON, M. (1989a) 'Setting the Scene' in HUGHES, J. J. (ed.) (1989) *AS Levels: Implications for Schools, Examining Boards and Universities.* London: The Falmer Press.

KINGDON, M. (1989b) 'Some Practical Issues for Chief Examiners' in HUGHES, J. J. (ed.) (1989) *AS Levels: Implications for Schools, Examining Boards and Universities.* London: The Falmer Press.

KINGDON, M.; WILMUT, J.; DAVIDSON, K. and ATKINS, S. B. (1986) *Report of the Inter-Board Comparability Study of Grading Standards in Advanced Level English: June 1984,* ULSEB on behalf of the GCE Boards of England, Wales and Northern Ireland.

KINGDON, M. and STOBART, G. (1988) *GCSE Examined.* London: The Falmer Press.

LAWTON, D. (1989) *Education, Culture and the National Curriculum.* London: Hodder and Stoughton.

LOVEDAY, S. (1989) 'Syllabus Developments', in HUGHES, J. J. (ed.) (1989) *AS Levels: Implications for Schools, Examining Boards and Universities.* London: The Falmer Press.

MACFARLANE, C. (1988) 'The Rise and Fall of General Studies', *Education,* 8 July, pp. 34–5.

MACLURE, S. (1988) *Education Re-formed.* London: Hodder and Stoughton.

NATIONAL CURRICULUM COUNCIL (1990) *Core Skills 16–19: a Response to the Secretary of State.* The Council.

THE NEEDS PROJECT (1988) *AS Level Survey 1: The Take Up and Implementation of AS Levels.* ULSEB/LEAG on behalf of the project.

161

THE NEEDS PROJECT (1989) *GCE–GCSE, An Update*, ULSEB/LEAG on behalf of the project.

NEWBOULD, C. A. and MASSEY, A. J. (1979) 'Comparability Using a Common Element', *Occasional Publication No. 7*. Cambridge: Test Development and Research Unit.

ORR, L. and NUTTALL, D. L. (1983) 'Determining Standards in the Proposed Single System of Examining at 16+', *Comparability in Examinations, Occasional Paper 2*. London: Schools Council.

ROBBINS, LORD (Chairman) (1963) *Higher Education: Report of the Committee under the Chairmanship of Lord Robbins*. London: HMSO.

SCHOOLS EXAMINATIONS AND ASSESSMENT COUNCIL (1989a) *Consultation on the Secretaries of State's Remit to the School Examinations and Assessment Council on the Promotion of AS Examinations and the Rationalisation of A Level Syllabuses: Report of the Findings*. London: The Council.

SCHOOL EXAMINATIONS AND ASSESSMENT COUNCIL (1989b) *Advanced and Advanced Supplementary Examinations: Factors Affecting the Promotion of AS Examinations*. London: The Council.

SCHOOL EXAMINATIONS AND ASSESSMENT COUNCIL (1990a) *Examinations Post-16: Developments for the 1990s*. London: The Council.

SCHOOL EXAMINATIONS AND ASSESSMENT COUNCIL (1990b) *General Principles of Advanced and Advanced Supplementary Examinations*. A series of draft internal SEAC papers.

SCHOOLS COUNCIL (1965) *Change and Response. The First Year's Work: October 1964–September 1965*. London: HMSO.

SCHOOLS COUNCIL (1966) *Sixth Form: Curriculum and Examinations*, Working Paper No. 5. London: HMSO.

SCHOOLS COUNCIL (1967a) *The New Curriculum*. London: HMSO.

SCHOOLS COUNCIL (1967b) *Some Further Proposals for Sixth Form Work*. Working Paper No. 16. London: HMSO.

SCHOOLS COUNCIL (1968) *Sixth Form Examining Methods*. Working Paper No. 20. London: HMSO.

SCHOOLS COUNCIL/STANDING CONFERENCE ON UNIVERSITY ENTRANCE (1969) *Report of the Joint Working Party on the Sixth Form Curriculum and Examinations, a report*. London: HMSO.

SCHOOLS COUNCIL (1972) *16–19: Growth and Response. No. 1 Curriculum Bases*, Working Paper No. 45. London: Evans/Methuen Educational.

SCHOOLS COUNCIL (1973a) *The Examination Courses of First Year Sixth Formers*, Schools Council Research Studies. London: Macmillan.

SCHOOLS COUNCIL (1973b) *16–19 Growth and Response. Examination Structure*, Working Paper No. 46. London: Evans/Methuen Educational.

SCHOOLS COUNCIL/SCUE (1973c) *Preparation for Degree Courses*, Working Paper No. 47. London: Evans/Methuen Educational.

SCHOOLS COUNCIL (1978a) *Examinations at 18+: the N and F Studies*, Working Paper No. 60. London: Evans/Methuen Educational.

SCHOOLS COUNCIL (1978b) *Examinations at 18+: Resource Implications of an N and F Curriculum and Examination Structure*, Examinations Bulletin No. 38. London: Evans/Methuen Educational.

SCHOOLS COUNCIL (1980) *Examinations at 18+: Report on the N and F Debate*, Working Paper No. 66. London: Methuen Educational.

SCRUTON, P. (1989) 'The Case for Breadth' in HUGHES, J. J. (ed.) (1989) *AS Levels: Implications for Schools, Examining Boards and Universities*. London: The Falmer Press.

SECONDARY EXAMINATIONS COUNCIL (1985a) *Annual Report 1984–5*. London: The Council.

SECONDARY EXAMINATIONS COUNCIL (1985b) *Reports of working parties draft grade criteria: English; Mathematics; Biology; Chemistry; Physics; Craft, Design and Technology; Geography; History; French; Welsh*. London: The Council.

SECONDARY EXAMINATIONS COUNCIL (1986) *Annual Report 1985–6*. London: The Council.

SECONDARY EXAMINATIONS COUNCIL (1987a) *Annual Report 1986–7*. London: The Council.

SECONDARY EXAMINATIONS COUNCIL (1987b) *Assessing modular syllabuses: A discussion document*, Working Paper No. 4. London: The Council.

SECONDARY EXAMINATIONS COUNCIL (1988) 'Modular Courses', *SEC News*, 9, pp. 1–2.

SECONDARY SCHOOLS EXAMINATION COUNCIL (1937) *The Higher School Certificate of Education*, The Council. London: HMSO.

SECONDARY SCHOOLS EXAMINATION COUNCIL (1943) *Curriculum and Examinations in Secondary Schools* (the Norwood Report), The Council, London: HMSO.

SECONDARY SCHOOLS EXAMINATION COUNCIL (1960) *Secondary School Examinations Other than the GCE: Report of a Committee Appointed by the Secondary School Examinations Council* (The Beloe Report), The Council. London: HMSO.

SECONDARY SCHOOL EXAMINATIONS COUNCIL (1962) *Sixth Form Studies and University Entrance Requirements*, Report No. 3. London: The Council.

SEYMOUR, R. and ACRES, D. (1987) *General Studies*. London: Longman.

STANDING CONFERENCE ON UNIVERSITY ENTRANCE (1987) *AS Levels and University Entrance* (revised edition). London: Committee of Vice-Chancellors and Principals.

STANDING COUNCIL ON UNIVERSITY ENTRANCE, SCHOOLS CURRICULUM DEVELOPMENT COMMITTEE, SECONDARY EXAMINATIONS COUNCIL AND COUNCIL FOR NATIONAL ACADEMIC AWARDS (1987) *Current Developments in School Curriculum and Examinations*. SCUE, SCDC, SEC, CNAA.

TIMES EDUCATIONAL SUPPLEMENT (1967) *Sixth Form Curriculum: New A Level Proposals*, 24 November, p. 1210.

TIMES EDUCATIONAL SUPPLEMENT (1989). *Ministers Unite in Search for a Common Core*, 1 December.

TURNER, R. H. (1960) 'Sponsored and Contest Mobility and the School System', *American Sociological Review*, 25, October, pp. 855–67.

UNIVERSITY OF LONDON (1946) *Regulations for the Session 1946–1947*. London: Matriculation and School Examinations Council.

UNIVERSITY OF LONDON SCHOOLS EXAMINATIONS BOARD (1986) *A*

Response to the Draft Grade Criteria. London: University of London School Examinations Board.

WARING, M. (1979) *Social Pressures and Curriculum Innovation.* London: Methuen.

WATKINS, P. (1989) 'Approaches in Some Schools and Colleges' in HUGHES, J. J. (ed.) (1989) *AS Levels: Implications for Schools, Examining Boards and Universities.* London: The Falmer Press.

WHITTACKER, R. J. and FORREST, G. M. (1983) *Problems of the GCE Advanced Level Grading System.* Manchester: The Joint Matriculation Board.

Index